the WEEKEND CRAFTER

BASKETRY

the WEEKEND CRAFTER

BASKETRY

17 GREAT WEEKEND PROJECTS

An Imprint of
Sterling Publishing Co., Inc.
New York

WWW.LARKCRAFTS.COM.

Dedication

For my mother, who taught me that the best way to get through a long project was one step at a time. And for my father, who taught me that the best way to get through a long project was with the right tools.

EDITOR:
JANICE EATON KILBY

ART DIRECTOR:
SUSAN MCBRIDE

ASSISTANT ART DIRECTOR & PRODUCTION:
HANNES CHAREN

PHOTOGRAPHY:
EVAN BRACKEN
(project photos)
ESTHER HOLSEN
(how-to photos)

ILLUSTRATIONS:
ORRIN LUNDGREN

EDITORIAL ASSISTANT:
NATHALIE MORNU

Library of Congress Cataloging-in-Publication Data

Crawford, BJ.
Basketry: 17 great weekend projects to make / BJ Crawford.
    p. cm. – (The weekend crafter)
Included index.
ISBN 978-1-4547-0179-8 (pb. : alk. paper)
1. Basket making. I. Title. II. Series.
TT879.B3C73 2011
746.41'2—dc21
                              2003002787
10 9 8 7 6 5 4 3 2 1

Published by Lark Crafts, A Division of
Sterling Publishing Co., Inc.
387 Park Avenue South, New York, NY 10016

First published in 2003 by Lark Books, A Division of Sterling Publishing Co., Inc.

Previously published as Basketry: 18 Easy & Beautiful Baskets to Make

© 2011 Lark Crafts, An Imprint of Sterling Publishing Co., Inc.
Text © 2003, BJ Crawford

Distributed in Canada by Sterling Publishing
c/o Candian Manda Group, 165 Dufferin Street
Toronto, Ontario, Canada M6K 3H6

Distributed in the United Kingdom by GMC Distribution Services,
Caste Place, 166 High Street, Lewes, East Sussex, England BN7 1XU

Distributed in Australia by Capricorn Link (Australia) Pty Ltd.,
P.O. Box 704, Windsor, NSW 2756 Australia

If you have questions or comments about this book, please contact:
Lark Crafts
67 Broadway
Asheville, NC 28801
828-253-0467

Manufactured in China

ISBN 13: 978-157990-331-2 (original edition) 978-1-4547-0179-8 (current edition)

For information about custom editions, special sales, premium and corporate purchases, please contact Sterling Special Sales Department at 800-805-5489 or specialsales@sterlingpub.com.

For information about desk and examination copies available to college anduniversity professors, requests must be submitted to academic@larkbooks.com. Our complete policy can be found at www.larkcrafts.com.

Immediate right:
DIANNE KENNEDY CRAVER,
Anna Kate (detail),
1998.

CONTENTS

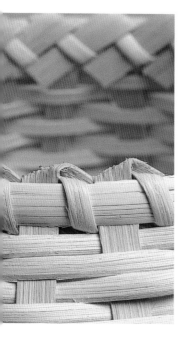

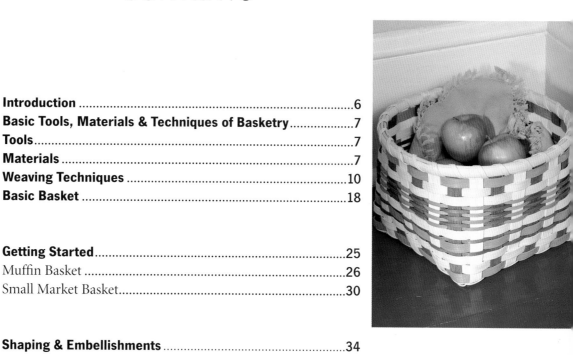

INTRODUCTION

Before people walked the earth, birds were our first basket weavers, interlacing fibers randomly but carefully for the protection and comfort of the next generation. No one human culture can be credited for the invention of baskets and no race or region can claim ownership, but all used containers to gather and carry, making what they needed from easily gathered materials. Adept fingers (and that astonishingly useful thumb) wove plant and animal fibers into usable shapes, each specific to its task. Many baskets were beautiful (a few very old examples remain), but most were products of form following function—the right size and shape for the job at hand. Today, plastic and paper bags do many of the jobs our ancestors' baskets did, and baskets have become purely decorative objects for most of us. But whether you build baskets for use or display, the thrill of making them takes us back to our roots. Basketry probably isn't the oldest profession, but you need only a few fingers to count the ones that make a better claim.

Making things has been central to my life. I learned to crochet when I was seven, to knit when I was 12, and made my own clothes by age 14. At 16, I designed and made costumes for a children's theater company and three years later became wardrobe supervisor for the Boston Ballet Company. In 1970, my extended family and I started Earth Guild, a craft material supply store in Massachusetts. We moved in 1976 to the mountains of western North Carolina, where Earth Guild is now located in the city of Asheville.

I started making baskets in 1971. My first attempts were rough, rather shapeless, and made mostly from coiled or twined fiber, so I called them "organic." (It *was* the early '70s.) There were very few books on basketry, almost no classes, and no on-line chat groups. Most of the books I found were either historical texts on American Indians (wonderful pictures of finished baskets but no step-by-step instructions) or woodcraft books for Boy Scouts (not very inspiring). I was on my own, reinventing the wheel, when Virginia Harvey's book, *The Techniques of Basketry*, was released in 1974. It opened

LINDA ARTER SURA, *Adrift,* 2001. 7" x 13" x 7" (17.8 x 33 x 17.8 cm); reed, driftwood. Photo by artist

up a new world for me. Since that time, I've been making baskets out of reed, hardwood splints, wire, and paper, as well as fibers.

My goal in this book is to open up the world of basketry to you too. With each basket that you make, your skills and confidence will increase. I've also included photos of dozens of beautiful baskets made by my friends, and I hope you get as much pleasure and inspiration as I do from looking at them.

BJ CRAWFORD, *Tall Black Urn,* 1996. 9" x 13" (22.9 x 33 cm); dyed flat, flat-oval, and round reed. Photo by Blair Logue

BASIC TOOLS, MATERIALS & TECHNIQUES OF BASKETRY

Tools

Basketry requires very few tools. Most are familiar household items and none are expensive. Here's all you need to get started:

- sharp gardening shears or household scissors for cutting
- pocketknife or craft knife for shaving
- paper shears for tapering
- different grades of sandpaper for smoothing
- awl or a fid to pry open spaces in the weave
- tape measure and pencil for marking
- needle-nose pliers for bending and folding
- round-nose pliers for grabbing
- clothespins, metal clips, or plastic cable ties to help hold things in place
- a bucket for soaking
- spray bottle to dampen materials as you work

The only tool you might not recognize is the *fid*. It's a leather-working tool the size of a small awl. Its blunt-tipped blade has a flat area in the middle. It's great for basketry and is one of my favorite tools. Of course, my own toolbox weighs at least 30 pounds (13.6 kg) because I find it necessary to own every clipper, poker, and clamp I find. But the truth is, I use only a fraction of the goodies in my box. Every basket maker has a special set of tools. Some can't work without a spoke weight, while others think specially made packing tools are essential. Deciding which are your personal favorites is part of the fun.

Materials

Baskets can be made from almost any flexible material, natural or not, including hardwood splints, vines, grasses, yarn, wire, and paper. The baskets in this book are made predominantly from *basket reed*. Reed is milled from the core of *rattan*, a member of the palm family (genus *Calamus*) that grows in the jungles of Indonesia, stretching along the forest floor and climbing into the trees. Harvesters chop the vines into 20- to 24-foot-long (6.1 to 7.3 m) poles 2 to 4 inches (5 to 10.2 cm) in diameter. Full-size poles or half-splits (poles split lengthwise down the middle) are used in rattan furniture. Poles are also die-cut into specific sizes, widths, and shapes of basket reed: round, flat, flat-oval, oval-oval, and half-round.

Reed is a natural material with all the irregularities that implies. Packaged in 1-pound (0.45 kg) coils or hanks, it's sold in craft supply shops and can be dyed or used in its natural light tan color. As you work through a coil, you'll find that each piece of reed is different. Some are stiff, some supple, some thicker, some thinner. Each has a use. Stiffer pieces are good for *stakes*, which form the frame of a basket, while more flexible pieces make better *weavers*.

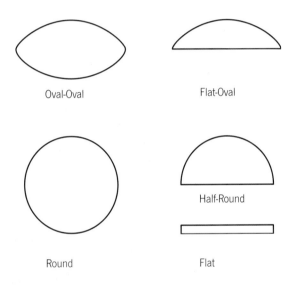

Oval-Oval

Flat-Oval

Round

Half-Round

Flat

Flat reed has a right side and a wrong side. The right side feels smooth, while the wrong side feels rough (it usually faces the inside of a basket). If you gently flex and bend the reed, little hairs will pop up on the rough side (photo above). It's usually easy to tell which side is which, but some pieces of reed feel smooth on both sides. The harder it is to tell, the less it matters, but always try to face the rougher side to the inside unless your pattern calls for the rough side out.

Flat-oval and *half-round* reed is flat on one side, rounded on the other. The flat side usually goes toward the inside of the basket, the rounded side out. *Oval-oval* has an almond shape and sharp edges, with both faces rounded.

Chair cane and binder cane are also rattan. They're cut from the outside layer of the rattan pole, the area between the bark and the center core. Because there's a limited amount of this layer on a pole, it usually costs more. Its outer side is slick and shiny.

TECHNIQUES FOR WORKING REED

Reed is always worked wet; three to five minutes of soaking is usually enough (it's very absorbent). Because rim pieces are thicker, they may need to soak for 10 to 15 minutes. Note that damp reed expands as it soaks up water. Therefore, pack the weavers very tightly against each other, because as the reed dries the spaces between the weavers will enlarge. Let the basket dry, then just before putting on the rim, give it a final packing, working from the bottom to the top.

The little hairs on the reed are the bane of basket makers. These annoying, tiny fibers that pop out all over the basket are the very thing that gives reed flexibility and strength, making it such good basket material. You will want them all to go away, but you can't avoid them completely. If you let the reed get too wet or work with it when it's too dry, you'll get more hairs. Rubbing pieces against each other too much causes hairs to pop out. Breathing hard creates hairs! But the more you work with the material, the more your hands will know what to do.

The flame from a Bunsen burner, gas stove, or canned cooking fuel will singe off hairs but also risks setting your basket on fire. Clipping hairs off a completed basket is easy but tedious. Sanding doesn't help at all and often raises more hairs. Avoiding them in the first place is the key. Clip off as many as you can from pieces before weaving. Never try to pull them off; it can ruin the reed. Try to place weavers between stakes without sliding them against each other, getting pieces into the right place the first time (a challenge for beginners). The more baskets you make, the fewer hairs you'll have. Practice doesn't always make perfect, but it nearly always improves.

HANDLING AND STORAGE

Reed usually comes tied in 1-pound (0.45 kg) coils. Carelessly opened, a coil of reed can explode into an unruly mess—especially round reed. Remove all the ties except for the one holding the ends of the reed together, and let the coil gradually unwind into a curly hank. Replace the remaining tie with a rubber band. When you pull a piece out of the bundle, have a friend hold the banded end (a window sash, closed drawer, or brick will also do the trick) while you gently jerk the piece loose from the other end, pulling it free without tangling.

Most baskets are made from more than one size of reed, and you rarely use a whole coil for any project. A coil of 1/2-inch (1.3 cm) flat-oval might be sufficient for

15 baskets, while a coil of ⅝-inch (1.6 cm) flat reed provides only enough for three. In short, you'll always have leftovers. Store reed in paper grocery bags, never plastic (the reed will mildew). I like to sort reeds by size and keep them in bags marked with the size, so I can keep track of what I have.

HANDLES

Adding a handle can completely change the character of a basket and enhance its usefulness.

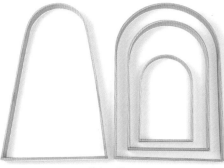

D handles

There are three basic handle shapes: *U*, *D*, and *swing handles*. *U handles* are added to a nearly finished basket just before the rim goes on. Some U handles have carved notches into which the rim locks, while unnotched ones are wrapped or glued in place. *D handles* are worked into the weave of the basket base from the very beginning and become part of the basket frame. *Swing handles* pivot, flopping down against the basket rim when not in use, making it easier to get things in and out of the basket. Swings are made either as U's (with or without notches) or D's. Most handles need a light sanding before being added to the basket. If you choose to add a light coat of wood finish (it's not a necessity), apply the finish before attaching the handles. Handle inserts are lighter-weight versions of U handles. They are never notched and are usually covered and wrapped.

Unless you need to alter the shape of a handle, they are not usually soaked. Some handles are glued with water-soluble glue and may come apart if left in water too long.

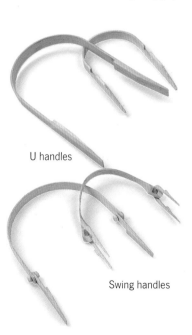

U handles

Swing handles

ALMA LAMBERT, *Lilly's Market Basket,* 1997 4½" x 10½" x 18" (11.4 x 26.7 x 45.7 cm); reed. Covered with braiding, a plain handle becomes something special. Photo by Evan Bracken

STAKES AND WEAVERS

Stakes are the pieces that form the bottom of a basket, then fold up to become the frame of the sides. Weavers are the pieces you weave through the stakes. Weavers usually follow an S curve around the stakes, which remain straight.

The project instructions are written for the right-handed. For many procedures, there's no significant difference, but lefties may find some things easier if they work in the reverse direction. For example, most righties weave in a counter-clockwise direction while many lefties are more comfortable going clockwise. Feel free to alter any instructions so they work for you.

DO-IT-YOURSELF COLOR

Though many suppliers sell dyed reed, it's easy and fun to dye your materials. Reed can be dyed with any household dye formulated to work on cotton. Different brands of dye can be made up from different pigments. The red from one supplier, for example, may differ from the red from another. It's hard to match colors exactly, and mixed colors get even trickier. The important thing is to end up with a color you like.

PATTI QUINN HILL,
The Wok (detail), 1999.
9" x 18" (22.9 x 45.7 cm);
rattan, wood.
Photo by artist

Weaving Techniques
Weave Structures

Plain weave is also called *simple weave* (1-1 weave). Because baskets originated in many places, the same process often has many names. In weaving shorthand, the first numeral stands for the number of stakes the weaver should pass over, and the second number stands for the stakes it should pass under. Therefore plain weave is plain, the simplest weave structure: over one then under one, over one then under one, for as long as it takes. The ins and outs of each row alternate with the row below. As they work up the sides of the basket (photo below), the weavers S curve around the stakes, which remain straight. In the bottom of a basket, the weave is often spaced out. Up the sides, the weavers are packed tightly together.

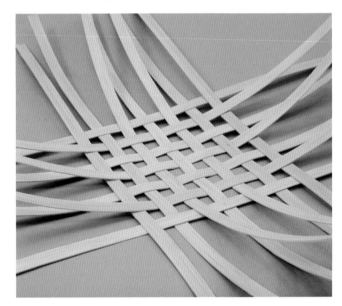

If you use basket dye, follow the directions on the package. If the dye lacks specific instructions for use with reed, a few general rules will get you through. Bundle the reed loosely and soak it in water for a little while. Put the damp reed in a container large enough to prevent crowding and pour the hot dye solution over it. The hotter the dye, the faster color develops. Let the reed steep until the dye has cooled. If you want to obtain an even color, take out the reed and rearrange it several times while the bath is cooling. Finally, rinse well.

You can dye a whole finished basket by using a container large enough to submerge the entire basket. Be careful of handles: glued joints may separate in hot water. You can usually reglue them if you catch it right away. The longer you wait, the greater the chance of warping and the harder it is to work the wood back into its original position. No dye is completely colorfast and all colors fade, especially if exposed to sunlight. Reed itself darkens naturally over time.

Some people like to finish a basket with a wood stain, oil finish, or even paint. I think baskets need to breathe and will live longer unsealed, but it's a matter of personal choice and the basket's intended use.

BJ CRAWFORD, *Shadow Weave Tray,* 1994. 14" x 18" x 4" (35.6 x 45.7 x 10.2 cm); dyed and natural reed. Varied sizes and colors of reed make this plain-weave tray look complex. Photo by Blair Logue

MARY YOUNG SMITH, *Morning Glory*, 1999. 6½" x 6" (16.5 x 15.2 cm); round reed. This beautiful basket incorporates wave-weave. Photo by Blair Logue

Triple-weave (also called *triple-twining* or *three-rod-wale*) is similar to twining, but you use three weavers instead of two, and weave each one over two then under one in alternation while twisting them around each other (photo above).

Twining (also called *pairing*) is often used to stabilize the base stakes and adds an interesting texture to the sides of a basket. Two weavers are worked alternately, making a twist in the space between the stakes (photo immediately above). Twining requires very flexible weaving material: yarns, twines, ropes, twisted grasses, or smaller sizes of round reed (photo above).

In *start-and-stop weave*, each row starts and ends in the same place, forming a single circuit. The beginning of the weaver is overlapped by the end of the same weaver for a distance of four stakes (photo immediately above). If the overlap is done properly, neither end of the weaver will be visible on the inside or outside of the basket.

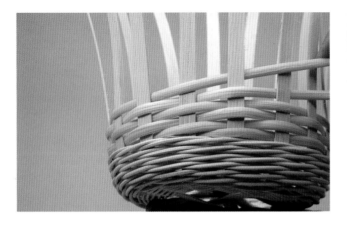

Chase-weave (or weave-and-chase) uses two weavers throughout. The weavers are long, not cut to any specific length, and they "chase" each other around the basket (photo above). Chasing is done over an even number of stakes. With flat or flat-oval weavers, you usually taper the ends by cutting down the width of each weaver so it eases into the woven body of the basket without a noticeable step. The two weavers begin on the same side of the basket, one just above the other, then are worked in a spiral up the basket (photo above). They don't twist, as weavers do in the process of twining. The upper weaver never passes the lower one.

Continuous weave is similar to chase-weave in that you weave in a spiral, but there is only one weaver. If you wish to create a continuous plain weave, you must work on an odd number of stakes so the weave alternates as you work up the sides. Most basket bases start out with an even number of stakes, so you'll either have to add a stake or split a stake by cutting it in half lengthwise.

Twill weaves are created over varying multiples of

stakes, depending on the desired pattern. You don't simply alternate successive rows. A 2-2 twill works over two stakes then under two stakes. But the next row steps over one stake in its placement, working 2-2 from that new starting point, forming diagonal patterns which ascend the sides of the basket like little stair steps (center right photo). Point twills change the direction of the slants, the weavers making little points where their directions change.

Twills may be either start-and-stop, continuous, or chase-weave. The number of stakes needed depends on the weave type and the specific pattern.

Start-and-stop twills can be quite complicated, building up beautiful patterns. The basketry of the Native American Cherokee culture includes stunning examples

of this weave structure. Fabric weaving pattern books are a good source for advanced twill patterns.

Continuous twills can be woven over an even or odd number of stakes, depending on the weave used. An even progression, such as 2-2 must be done on an odd number of stakes. An odd weave, such as 2-1, is done on a multiple of three stakes, plus or minus one. In other words, the weave advances or recedes by one stake on each successive round.

PATTI HAWKINS, *Out of the Darkness*, 1999. 11" x 10" (27.9 x 25.4 cm); rattan, waxed linen. Photo by Boyd-Fitzgerald Photography

PATTI HAWKINS, *Destiny*, 2000. 11" x 10" (27.9 x 25.4 cm); rattan, waxed linen. Photo by Boyd-Fitzgerald Photography

PATTI HAWKINS, *Trinity*, 2001. 18" x 18" (45.7 x 45.7 cm); rattan, waxed linen. Photo by Boyd-Fitzgerald Photography

ADDING ON NEW WEAVERS

When weaving any of the spiral weaves (twining, chase, or continuous) you'll eventually have to add weavers. Add flat and flat-oval reed by overlapping four stakes (photo above right).

Adding on to round reed weavers is a bit more complicated. You can begin and end weavers behind the same stake or hide them inside the basket wall. The first method is easier but leaves pointy ends on the basket's interior (photo left). The second solution is more difficult but results in a tidier basket. End the weaver by folding it at the left side of a stake and tucking it down into the little pocket formed by the twining below (lower left photo). Use the same technique to add the new weaver to the right of the preceding stake.

When twill-weaving, add to a weaver as you would for plain weave but overlap the weavers a little more. That way you'll catch the ends securely.

PATTI QUINN HILL, *Bowl of Blue Spirals*, 1999. 8" x 17" (20.3 x 43.2 cm); rattan, wood. High color contrast shows off the weave structure of this spiral twill bowl. Photo by artist

SHAPING

No matter what weave structure you use, *you* control the basic shape of the basket—in theory. For beginning basket makers, it can be a struggle to make the intended shape happen. Fortunately, the more baskets you build, the easier shaping becomes. Just keep your desired shape in mind and gently encourage the weavers and stakes toward the places you want them to be. Remember: no two baskets are alike. Each will have its own personality.

PATTI QUINN HILL, *Spirals In & Out*, 1999. 10" x 18" (25.4 x 45.7 cm); rattan, wood. This basket is an exceptional example of shaping as well as color contrast. Photo by artist

BASES

Bases are the starting points for all splint baskets. They can be plain-woven or twill-woven, spoked or Nantucket, open weave or filled. The weave structure is determined by the specific basket pattern you're making. Plain-weave bases feature a simple plain pattern. Twill-woven bases follow a specific twill pattern (often 2-2), with each successive row stepping one stake ahead. The stakes in round bases make a starburst pattern. A Nantucket basket base (circular, square, or oval) starts from a solid wood center with a grove in the edge into which stakes are pushed. Filled bases contain extra pieces which are woven in to close the gaps in an open-weave base. Those pieces don't become part of the side structure, however.

PACKING

As you weave in new weavers, you must also pack them by pushing down the weavers against each other. This process is very important, and if done properly, will make your basket tight, pretty, and even. Some people pack with their fingers, some with tools. I do both depending on the basket. Either way, the idea is to push down the weavers as tight as you can. Most basket-weaving materials are worked wet and have expanded; this is especially true of hardwoods such as ash and oak, as well as reed. The weavers shrink as they dry, gaps appearing between them. If I have time, I let the basket dry overnight and give it one last packing before adding the rim.

DIANNE KENNEDY CRAVER, *Anna Kate*, 1998. 18" x 10" x 10" (45.7 x 25.4 x 25.4 cm); natural and dyed reed, wood. A bushel-style handle added at the widest point makes this basket easy to carry and use. Photo by Evan Bracken

Some reshaping can be done after a basket is finished. If the bottom isn't flat, put a weight on the rim while it dries. If a basket is a little off-center, press against the sides to reform them. Plus, you can always face a basket's wobbly side toward the wall!

Shaker and Nantucket Lightship baskets are usually woven around specially made wood molds. Though a mold makes shaping easier, it limits you to that particular shape. This book contains a basket inspired by those traditions, but you won't need a mold to make it.

RIMS

My fellow basket maker and friend Blair Logue says a basket without a rim is like a skirt without a hem. A rim is what makes baskets look finished and clean. It's usually a thicker material, often flat-oval or half-round reed, attached to the top edge with *lashing* (stitching). Before the rim is lashed in place, a *rim filler* is often added to the basket's top edge to smooth and even it out. Filler can be round reed, seagrass, a twist of waxed linen, or another material flexible enough to follow the curve of the top edge

of the basket. Many basket makers dislike putting on rims, because it's hard to pull everything snug, especially if you've just finished weaving a whole basket. If you want the satisfaction of finishing the basket in one afternoon, you can add the rim right away, but it isn't necessary. I like to wait overnight before adding the rim; my hands aren't tired and I can pack the sides tightly before beginning the rim.

I use plastic cable ties instead of clothespins or clips to hold rim pieces in place for lashing. Ties can be pulled very tight and won't slip. The drawback is that they can only be used once. Reusable ties exist but they don't hold as well.

Plastic Milk Carton Slides and Guides

Here's a trick a friend shared with me that makes tucking stakes much easier. Cut a piece of a plastic milk jug a little wider than the width of your stakes and 6 inches (15.2 cm) long; fold it in half. Cut a point on the folded  end, leaving about ¼ inch (6 mm) still attached at the fold . Push down the folded plastic into the side wall of the basket, where the stake is supposed to be tucked. Pull apart the two layers and push in the stake. The smooth surface of the plastic helps the reed slide in. Now use your awl to grab the fold in the plastic and pull it down and out. Slick! See the photo immediately below.

LASHING

Lashing is the "stitching" that keeps all the rim pieces in place, and baskets can be lashed with anything long and flexible. Smaller sizes of round reed or waxed thread work, but lashing is usually done with narrow flat or flat-oval reed. Sometimes cane is used; it has a glossy finish and can be a nice addition to the basket design.

Always point the end of your lashing to help it slide into the place it needs to go more easily. There are also many types of lashing guides, which help open a space for the lashing. A piece of a plastic milk jug does the

same trick. Cut a guide a little wider than your lashing. Push it into the little space through which the lashing will go. Slide the lashing between the layers of plastic, slipping it into place.

Sometimes it's hard to get the lashing tight enough. You can go back and give it one last tightening before you hide the ends. Use your fid or awl for leverage as shown below.

OVERLAY TECHNIQUES

Cross-stitching and curls are overlay techniques. They have nothing to do with the structure of the basket but are added after completion. They provide texture and interest that can make a simple basket fancy. You'll learn how to do them later in the book.

DIANNE KENNEDY CRAVER, *Lattice Work*, 2000. 7" x 8" x 10" (17.8 x 20.3 x 25.4 cm); natural and dyed reed. Space-dyed reed adds to the liveliness of this basket's cross-stitch ornamentation. Photo by Evan Bracken

JESSIE STEWART, *Market Basket*, 1995. 11" x 17" x 8" (27.9 x 43.2 x 20.3 cm); dyed and natural reed, hand-carved handle. A "Cherokee Wheels" overlay created from round reed enhances this simple market basket. Design by Patricia Yunkes. Photo by Blair Logue

SUBSTITUTIONS

The how-to projects include lists of specific materials, but you can often substitute sizes. Stakes should never differ from their specified dimensions by more than $^1/_8$ inch (3 mm), but weavers can be almost any size or color. If the pattern calls for a $^1/_4$-inch (6 mm) piece for lashing, but you have a whole coil of $^3/_{16}$-inch (4.5 mm) flat-oval, the smaller material will probably work just fine. As you'd do with a cooking recipe, make the first basket with the materials specified, then experiment with other choices.

EMBELLISHMENTS

You can embellish a basket with anything: beads, feathers, bells, ribbon, bones, or fur, to name a few. You can work them into the weaving or sew them on after the fact. Suddenly a plain basket transforms into an outstanding one.

ALMA LAMBERT, *Gift Basket*, 2000. 4¾" x 4" x 9" (12.1 x 10.2 x 22.9 cm); reed. The simple addition of a button and bow can change the entire feel of a basket. Photo by Evan Bracken

SHANNON WEBER, *Raven Sings*, 1999. 36" x 17" x 15" (92.7 x 43.2 x 38.1 cm); rattan, black walnut dye, leather, tin, glass beads, turquoise button with silver inlay. Embellishment, color, and shaping work beautifully together in this basket. Photo by Rick Hiser

THERE'S NOTHING COMPLETELY NEW UNDER THE SUN

The projects in this book are my personal designs, in that I've chosen the techniques and materials and sizes to create them. This doesn't mean other craftspeople haven't had similar ideas. It's very unlikely that a designer would create a totally new basket, because the craft of basketry is spread over too many centuries and continents. I've woken up with a great idea only to find it was done thousands of years ago in India or China. A market basket is, after all, just a basket for marketing. What you can do as a designer is rearrange the pieces of the puzzle. On a good day, you'll end up with something that pleases you.

How to Use this Book

The book is structured to be used in different ways. If you're a new basketmaker, start with the Basic Basket on page 18 to learn fundamental basketry techniques. Then, work your way through the other types of baskets to learn new techniques and acquire additional skills. Or, if you're the adventurous type or have experience with basketmaking, feel free to begin with any project in the book; handy references will direct you to the basic information you'll need to know in order to make that basket.

My goal in this book is to open up the world of basketry to you, too. With each basket that you make, your skills and confidence will increase. I've also included photos of dozens of beautiful baskets made by my friends, and I hope you get as much pleasure and inspiration as I do from looking at them.

Basic Basket

The Basic Basket is designed to teach beginners the fundamental process of making a basket. As you make this small, square basket, you'll learn several major steps.

MATERIALS			
QUANTITY	MATERIAL & DIMENSIONS	LENGTH	FUNCTION
14	$1/2$" (1.3 cm) flat reed	20" (50.8 cm)	stakes
1	#2 round reed	12' (3.6 m)	twining
6	$1/4$" (6 mm) flat-oval reed	33" (83.8 cm)	weavers
3	$1/2$" (1.3 cm) flat reed	33" (83.8 cm)	weavers
1	$3/8$" (9.5 mm) flat reed	33" (83.8 cm)	hidden weaver
2	$3/8$" (9.5 mm) flat-oval reed	33" (83.8 cm)	rim
1	#3 seagrass	33" (83.8 cm)	rim filler
1	$1/4$" (6 mm) flat-oval reed	7' (2.1 m)	lashing

INSTRUCTIONS

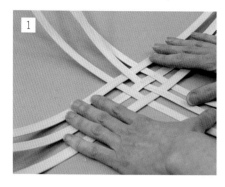

1 Laying out and Weaving the Base

A base can be laid out many ways. You can arrange all the horizontal stakes, holding them down with a spoke weight, then weave in the vertical pieces. I like to start in the center and work out from that point (photo 1). Whatever you do, be sure that every stake is centered and all the wrong sides face up (or down, if your pattern calls for it).

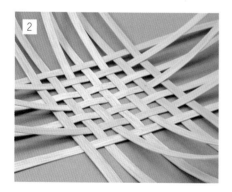

Start by marking the center of each stake on its wrong (rough) side. Soak the stakes briefly. Use all 14 pieces, seven in each direction, to weave the bottom in a simple plain weave. Match the center points, making sure the wrong sides of the stakes face up. Your base should look like photograph 2.

2 Sizing and Squaring the Base

Adjust the woven pieces to create a 6 1/2 x 6 1/2-inch (16.5 x 16.5 cm) square, the stakes evenly spaced. Up to now, you've focused on the weave structure. Now pull back and look at the base as a whole. Check that the pieces are centered, the weave pattern has no mistakes, and the rough side of the reed faces up. Finally, to ensure a square base rather than a parallelogram, check that the corner-to-corner, diagonal measurements are equal. Mark the corners (photo 3) so you can correct the placement if something slips.

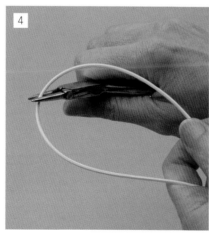

3 Twining

Now you'll twine two rows around the base. Use round-nose pliers to fold a weaver not quite in half, leaving one end a little longer than the other. That way, if you have to add more weavers, the joining won't be in exactly the same place. Crush the fold point of the reed (photo 4) so it folds without cracking. Slip the loop

formed by the fold around any stake that's underneath another stake (photo 5).

You now have two weavers with which to work. Start with the left weaver. Weave it over the stake to the right, under the next stake, and out to the surface of the basket (photo 6). Pick up the other weaver (now on the left). Repeat the same weave: over one/under one/out. Make sure you always work on top of (over) the leading weaver (photo 7). Put down that piece and weave with the other piece (which is again the leftmost). Continue this alternation, weaving around the basket, packing the twining tightly against the sides of the base. Keep the stakes flat and straight as you work. The weavers should curve around the stakes, spacing them out and holding them in place. There will be a twist, which is characteristic of the weave called twining, between the stakes.

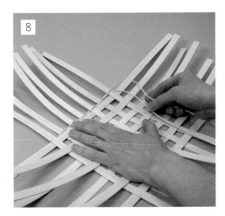

4 Making the Corners

Weaving around corners can be a bit confusing at first. Continue alternating the weavers around the corner stakes; don't let the stakes slip as you work around them. Always work the left weaver over (on top of, to the outside of) the leading one (photo 8). Snug the twining against the edge of the base and square the corner (photo 9).

When you've completed two rounds of twining, slip the ends down between the layers of the stakes (photo 10). Clip off the ends to hide them.

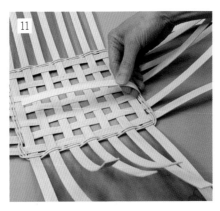

5 Upsetting

In the process of *upsetting* or *upstaking*, you turn up the stakes from the base to form the sides and lock them in place with the first few rows of weaving. This is often the most difficult step in making a basket. (Maybe *that's* why it's called upsetting!)

The first part is easy. Dampen the base to help the stakes fold without cracking too badly. Gently fold each stake over the side edge of the base (photo 11). The hard part is keeping the stakes upright. They won't want to stay put, but it's important to entice them into an upright position. It's okay if they crack slightly along the fold line, as long as they don't break completely.

Turning up can be accomplished with many different weaving techniques. For the Basic Basket, you'll use *start-and-stop weave*.

6 Turning up the Sides (Using Start-and-Stop Weave)

Every basket has its point of greatest frustration, when you think you're going to end up with a little tangle of kindling rather than a basket. Many beginners reach this point when weaving the first few rows up the sides. Hang in there. It does get easier.

Many of the baskets in this book are turned up with start-and-stop weave. Since it takes two to three rows to make the stakes stay upright, you can use lots of clips to hold the first weaver in place. I also like to work with two weavers and a *brake*. The brake is a scrap of reed (it can even be round) that's a little longer than one side of your basket. It's used to keep the stakes in place on the first side of the basket and is removed when the second row of weaving reaches around to the side with the brake.

Your first row of start-and stop weave should alternate with the base weave, regardless of any twining. You need a four-stake overlap to lock that row in place, so start two or three stakes in from the left-hand corner. That way, you won't have a double layer of reed around the corners. Whether you start at the second or third stake depends on the base weave; remember, you have to alter-

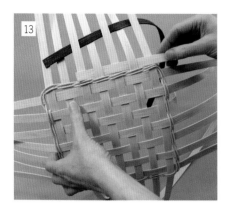

nate. Start on the outside of a stake to make it easier to end the row. Locate the appropriate stake. Place the end of the weaver flush with the left side of that stake. The right side of the reed should face the outside of the basket. Work over and under the stakes along that side of the basket (photo 12).

To hold the stakes in place, add the brake above the weaver in the alternate pattern. Don't jam the brake tightly against the first weaver; use just enough pressure to hold things in place (photo 13).

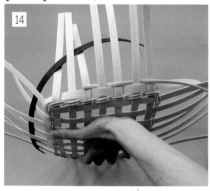

Weave the first weaver around the corner and along the second side. Now start the second weaver just above the first but in the alternate over-under pattern. Pack it down tightly against the first weaver (photo 14). Continue weaving around the basket, using the bottom weaver first, then the second (like chase-weave, discussed on page 12).

When you reach the side where you started, remove the brake and slip the end of the bottom weaver over (outside) its beginning point. This is the point where things want to spring apart; a few clips will help. Trim off the weaver to a length that overlaps four stakes, ending on the right side of the fourth stake (photo 15). If the overlap is done correctly, the weaver's ends will be hidden on the inside and outside of the basket.

Now weave the second weaver over that joining, ending it with a four-stake overlap on the side where it began (photo 16). Pack both of these pieces tightly against the bottom of the basket.

Start each successive row on a different side of the basket to maintain an even wall thickness. For this kind of weave, I like to cut all of my weavers to a specific length that's a little longer than needed. This helps with shaping, although it's more wasteful than cutting the weavers after they're woven in place. If you cut off more and more of the weavers as you work up the sides of the basket, you'll pull each row a little tighter, causing the sides of the basket to slope in. If a little less is cut from each weaver, the basket will flare out. You may want either of these things

to happen, but it should be under your control.

This is where the fun begins, because from now on you can weave in one piece at a time. I still remember the thrill I experienced when my first set of unruly stakes turned itself into a container. You can add the weavers in the order shown in photograph 17) or be creative and change the order around.

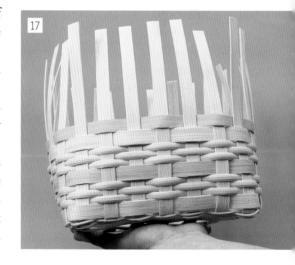

7 Adding the Hidden (False) Weaver

Before adding the rim pieces, you must weave in the top rim row. Many basket makers call this the *false weaver*, but I like to call it the *hidden weaver* because it's hidden by the outer rim pieces and isn't false at all. It's usually woven in a start-and-stop weave woven with flat reed that's a little narrower than the flat-oval rim pieces (top row of weaving shown in photo 17). Next, tightly pack down all of the weavers, making sure the basket's top edge is level.

8 Folding and Tucking the Stakes

To hold the rim in place, you must fold some of the stakes over the hidden weaver and tuck them down into the inside wall of the basket. If you simply clipped off all of the stakes at the top edge, the rim could be pulled off. Some basket makers fold all the stakes. The ones ending on the inside of the hidden weaver fold to the outside while the others fold to the inside. Except in very specific cases, I only fold the ones ending on the outside and clip off the others.

Start by clipping off the stakes that end on the inside of the hidden weaver (photo 18). It's not necessary to clip them off with great precision at this point. In fact, it's easier to even them up with the top edge after the others are turned and out of the way.

Wet the outside stakes and fold them over the hidden weaver (photo 19). It doesn't matter if they crack and splinter a bit. The rim filler will go on top, covering them up.

Clip off the stakes at an angle so they're just long enough to catch under two or three weavers. Slip the end of each stake down into the inside wall of the basket between the stake and the weavers, using your awl or fid to open a space for the insertion (photo 20). First, fold and tuck one stake on each side of the basket to hold the top edge level. Once those

four are set, continue folding and tucking in any order until all the stakes are done. See page 15 for tips.

Now that the tucked stakes are out of the way, clip the others flush with the rim. Because of the angle of the scissors, it's easier to work from the inside of the basket.

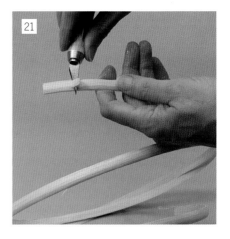

9 Scarfing the Rim Pieces

The rim is formed from two pieces of ³/₈-inch (9.5mm) flat-oval reed. One piece goes on the inside of the hidden weaver and one piece on the outside, flat sides against the hidden weaver. Position the seagrass rim filler along the top edge between the two flat-oval pieces. All of these pieces should overlap with themselves about the length of two stakes. Measure the length of the rim pieces and use a knife to thin down one end, removing some of the bulk (photo 21). This shaving process is called *scarfing*.

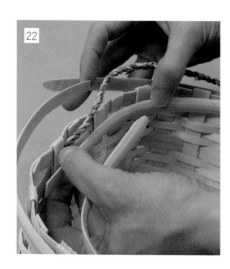

avoid shredding the lashing. Pull one end inside the basket so it's about 2 feet (.61 m) longer than the end outside. The flat (or rough) side of the lashing should end up against the rim pieces.

I like to position all three overlaps (filler, inner flat-oval, and outer flat-oval) in different places on the same side of the basket (photo 22). Many basket makers put the overlaps on different sides. I think it's easier to adjust them if they're adjacent but not in exactly the same place or things will get too bulky. Use cable ties or clips to attach the pieces to the basket.

10 Lashing the Rim

Now you'll use lashing to secure the rim pieces. I start the lashing at the center point of the side of the basket across from the overlaps, working around to the left with half of the lashing piece and to the right with the other half, so the two ends meet just past the overlapping rim pieces. This way, I have to pull only half of the length of the lashing through the basket each time, saving effort and wear on the lashing. Before starting, I also cut off each end of the lashing at an angle, creating a point to thread with.

To begin, pull the lashing through the space formed by the rim pieces and two adjacent stakes, just under the rim (photo 23), while using the fid or awl to open up the space to

Wrap the inside section of lashing around the rim pieces, then diagonally across and into the next hole to the right (photo 24). Use the awl or fid to open up the hole. Make sure the lashing isn't twisted, then pull it tight, wrap it around the rim, and feed it through the next hole.

Continue lashing with this piece until you reach the overlaps, then stop. Start lashing with the other end in the other direction. When you work in one direction, the lashing passes from outside to inside. When you work in the other direction, it goes from the inside to the outside.

Stop when you again reach the overlapped section.

Now scarf and round off the other ends of the rim pieces, as shown in photo 25.

Splice the seagrass filler into a tidy circle by cutting off a portion of the ply and twisting the longer fibers over each other (photo 26).

Work the longer end of the lashing across the overlaps until the two ends of lashing pass through the same space, one on the inside and one on the outside (photo 27, next page). As you work over the ends of the seagrass, poke them down in between the walls of the rim.

11 Finishing the Basket

Go back and make sure the lashing is tight. Now you'll finish off the ends of lashing by locking them in place under the rim pieces. The outside piece goes up on the outside of the hidden weaver (photo 28), then back down on the inside (photo 29). Yes, it goes under all of the rim pieces. Now clip off the end of the lashing you've just hidden at the base of the inside rim (photo 30).

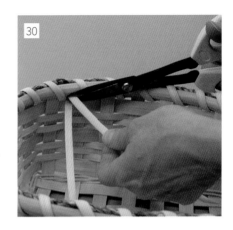

The inside piece of lashing follows a similar path but goes up on the inside (photo 31) and down on the outside (photo 32). Now clip the tail off the second piece at the bottom of the rim. Your Basic Basket is finished. Hey, you're a basket maker!

GETTING STARTED

The two baskets that follow are intended to build the skills you'll need to work through the other baskets in this collection. You're welcome, of course, to start with any project in this book, including the more challenging ones, but you may have to refer to earlier pages to find instructions for a particular technique. However, if you're new to basket making, I recommend that you make the Basic Basket (page 18) before attempting any of the projects.

(Top of page) **DIANNE KENNEDY CRAVER**, *Ode to Joy*, 1994. $12^1/2$" x $12^1/2$" (31.8 x 31.8 cm); natural and dyed reed, bushel-style side handles, twill weave accents. Photo by Evan Bracken

(Directly above) **MARY YOUNG SMITH**, *Double Play*, 2000. $7^1/2$" x $7^1/2$" (19 x 19 cm); flat and round reed. Photo by Blair Logue

Muffin Basket

*With this handsome basket, you'll learn how to use stakes of different
lengths and to insert and wrap a handle. Because of the handle,
the lashing is a little different, too.*

BASIC SKILLS NEEDED

laying out a base, page 19

twining, page 19

upsetting, page 20

start-and-stop plain weave, page 21

adding a rim, page 22

lashing, page 23

TECHNIQUES YOU'LL LEARN

making a handle

wrapping a handle

FINISHED SIZE 7 X 10 X 4 INCHES
(17.8 X 25.4 X 10.2 CM), NOT INCLUDING
HANDLE HEIGHT

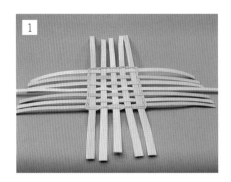

INSTRUCTIONS

1 Mark the stakes on their wrong (rough) sides, at their centers and in a way to help you differentiate among the different lengths. Soak the stakes just long enough to make them pliable. Lay out the bottom of the basket in a plain weave (photo 1). The five 21-inch (53.3 cm) stakes go in one direction, the six 19-inch (48.3 cm) stakes plus the much longer handle stake go in the other. Rough sides face up. Position the handle stake

MATERIALS

QUANTITY	MATERIAL & DIMENSIONS	LENGTH	FUNCTION
5	⁵/₈" (1.6 cm) flat reed	21" (53.3 cm)	stakes
6	⁵/₈" (1.6 cm) flat reed	19" (48.3 cm)	stakes
1	⁵/₈" (1.6 cm) flat reed	44" (111.8 cm)	handle stake
1	#2 round reed	10' (3 m)	twining
3	⁵/₈" (1.6 cm) flat reed	30" (76.2 cm)	weavers
7	¹/₄" (6 mm) flat-oval reed	30" (76.2 cm)	weavers
1	³/₈" (9.5 mm) flat reed	30" (76.2 cm)	hidden weaver
1	³/₄" (1.9 cm) handle insert	17" (43.2 cm)	handle
1	¹/₄" (6 mm) flat-oval reed	18" (45.7 cm)	handle overlay
1	¹/₄" (6 mm) flat-oval reed	7' (2.1 m)	handle wrap
2	¹/₂" (1.3 cm) flat-oval reed	30" (76.2 cm)	rim
1	#3 seagrass	30" (76.2 cm)	rim filler
1	¹/₄" (6 mm) flat-oval reed	7' (2.1 m)	lashing

underneath the middle 21-inch (53.3 cm) stake and center it between the 19-inch (48.3 cm) stakes, three stakes on either side. Center everything and adjust the bottom to a dimension of 5$\frac{1}{2}$ x 7$\frac{1}{2}$ inches (14 x 19 cm). Mark the corners. Using the #2 round reed, twine two rounds around the base.

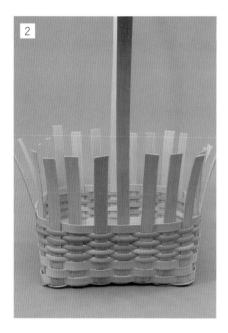

2 Now you'll use start-and-stop weave to upsett the stakes. Fold and crimp the stakes at the edge of the basket base, then use the $\frac{5}{8}$-inch (1.6 cm) flat and the $\frac{1}{4}$-inch (6 mm) flat-oval reed to weave up the sides of the basket, smooth sides facing outward. You may weave these pieces up the sides in any order you choose. I put the wide weavers at the bottom and the narrower ones above (photo 2). The basket shape is fairly simple; try to keep the side walls straight as you work up. Use the piece of $\frac{3}{8}$-inch (9.5 mm) flat reed as the hidden weaver to weave the last row. Adjust the sides and make everything even.

3 Fold and tuck the outside stakes to the inside and clip off the inside stakes—but don't clip off the handle stake. To make the handle, push one end of the handle stake into the opposite wall of the basket, adjusting it to the desired height. Cut a point on one end of the handle insert and slip it down against the handle stake. Cross the remaining end of the handle stake over the top of the insert and down along its side (photo 3). Adjust all the pieces to the same height. If desired, clip the handle overlay of $\frac{1}{4}$-inch (6 mm) flat-oval reed to the outside of all the handle pieces for more visual interest.

4 Slip the end of the handle wrap into the inside wall of the basket behind the handle. Make sure the flat (wrong) side is against the handle (photo 4).

5 Wrap the 1/4-inch (6 mm) flat-oval reed around the handle, catching all the pieces together. Wrap in a spiral, weaving over and under the handle overlay as desired (photo 5). When you reach the other side of the handle, slip the end of the wrapping down into the inside wall of the basket, and neatly clip off the end of the overlay.

7 Take the same end up to the left of the handle, down across the front, and into the hole below the rim to the right of the handle. You've now created an X over the rim at the handle (photo 7).

8 Using the end of the lashing on the right side of the handle, lash around to the overlaps on the opposite side, pulling everything snug. Stop at the overlaps and hold the lashing in place with a clothespin.

9 Use the other end of the lashing to lash around the other side.

10 Scarf and shape the rim so it overlaps smoothly. Use the longer piece of lashing to work across the overlaps. Make an X over this side of the handle as you did in step 7 and continue lashing until the two ends meet. Finish off the ends of the lashing.

6 Now you'll create a rim like that of the Basic Basket, but with an X formed around the handle. You'll use the two pieces of 1/2-inch (1.3 cm) flat-oval reed to form the rim plus the seagrass filler, all fitted to the top edge and held in place with cable ties. I like to put the overlaps on either side of the handle, not right on top of it. The seagrass will be placed to the outside of the handle, to be spliced anywhere along the same side as the overlaps. Soak the piece of 1/4-inch (6 mm) flat-oval reed for a minute. Start the lashing at the handle on the side of the basket where there are no overlaps. Thread the lashing into the hole just below the rim and to the left of the handle, pulling it through until the end inside the basket is 2 feet (61 cm) longer than the end outside. Run the inside lashing diagonally behind the handle and up to the right, making sure the rounded side of the flat-oval reed faces out. Take the end that's now to the right of the handle, cross it over the front of the rim and into the same hole where you started, just below the rim and to the left of the handle (photo 6).

Small Market Basket

This basket is called a market basket because of its shape and the integration of the handle with the bottom, which strengthens the whole basket and makes it useful for shopping. This project is very similar to the Muffin Basket, but you'll insert the handle into the base, making it a little more difficult—especially when you twine around the base. It's decorated with dyed reed, which you can buy ready-made or dye yourself.

BASIC SKILLS NEEDED

laying out a base, page 19

twining, page 19

upsetting, page 20

start-and-stop plain weave, page 21

adding a rim, page 23

lashing, page 23

TECHNIQUES YOU WILL LEARN

adding a D handle

FINISHED SIZE 6 X 12 X 5 INCHES
(15.2 X 30.5 X 12.7 CM),
NOT INCLUDING HANDLE HEIGHT

OTHER SUPPLIES

light and dark blue basket dye

MATERIALS

QUANTITY	MATERIAL & DIMENSIONS	LENGTH	FUNCTION
5	$5/8$" (1.6 cm) flat reed	26" (66 cm)	long stakes
8	$5/8$" (1.6 cm) flat reed	21" (53.3 cm)	stakes
1	D handle 6" x 10" (15.2 x 25.4 cm)		handle
1	#2 round reed	12' (3.6 m)	twining
5	$1/2$" (1.3 cm) flat reed	38" (96.5 cm)	weavers*
4	$1/4$" (6 mm) flat-oval reed	38" (96.5 cm)	weavers**
1	$3/4$" (1.9 cm) flat reed	38" (96.5 cm)	weaver
1	$3/8$" (9.5 mm) flat reed	38" (96.5 cm)	hidden weaver
2	$1/2$" (1.3 cm) flat-oval reed	38" (96.5 cm)	rim
1	#3 seagrass	38" (96.5 cm)	rim filler
1	$3/16$" (5 mm) flat-oval reed	10' (3 m)	lashing

*2 are dyed dark blue **all are dyed light blue

INSTRUCTIONS

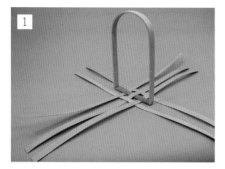

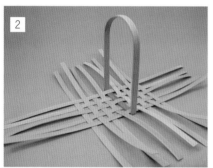

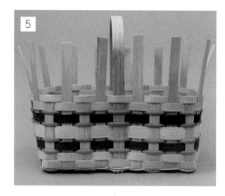

4 Use the $^1/_2$-inch (1.3 cm) flat reed, the $^1/_4$-inch (6 mm) flat-oval reed, and the $^3/_4$-inch (1.9 cm) flat reed to weave up the sides of the basket. Weave the different weavers up the sides in any order desired. I put the $^3/_4$-inch (1.9 cm) piece in the middle, but it's your choice.

1 Mark the centers of the 13 stakes on their wrong (rough) sides. Work materials damp. Lay out the bottom of the basket in a plain weave with the five 26-inch (66 cm) stakes in one direction and the eight 21-inch (53.3 cm) stakes plus the handle in the other direction. The handle should be in the middle of its set and all stakes facing wrong side up. The center 26-inch (66.0 cm) stake should lie on top of the handle (photo 1), so the first round of weaving will run along the outside of the handle. Weave in all the stakes, adjusting the bottom to $5^1/_2$ x $9^1/_2$ inches (14 x 24.1 cm). Make sure the base is square and all stakes are centered (photo 2). Mark the corners.

2 Twine two rows around the base. When you reach the handle, treat it as another stake (photo 3). Hide the twining's ends between the layered stakes. The completed base should look like photograph 4.

3 Fold and crimp the stakes at the edge of the basket base, and use start-and-stop weave to upsett them.

5 Use the $^3/_8$-inch (9.5 mm) flat reed to weave the last row of the basket. Adjust the sides, tightly packing them and making everything even (photo 5).

6 Fold and tuck the outer stakes to the inside, and clip off the inner stakes.

7 Attach the rim as you did in the Muffin Basket (page 29), making an X at the handle. Finish off the ends of the lashing.

Designing Your Own Market Basket

Would you like to make a market basket in a different size? The chart below will help. It gives starting points for several different-size baskets: the width, length, and number of stakes, and approximate dimensions and heights. Because there's nothing more frustrating than getting part way around and running out, the weavers, twining, and lashing allowances are extra long. Trim them as needed. Increase the length of the lashing if you'd like to do something more elaborate than a simple single lashing stitch.

The measurements are meant to be guidelines and jumping-off points to help you design your own baskets. Your basket can be taller or shorter as you choose. Remember: the inside width of a handle determines the exact width of the base regardless of the measurements. Weave up the sides with any combination of reed widths and types (weaver lengths are longer than you'll need). If you can't find twining material long enough for the larger baskets, start with two pieces instead of folding one longer piece in half. Piece rim lashing if desired by hiding the ends under the rim (page 24).

BASKET BASE	HANDLE SIZE	STAKE WIDTH	QUANTITY OF STAKES	LENGTH	QUANTITY OF STAKES	LENGTH
3" x 5" (7.6 x 12.7 cm)	3" x 4" (7.6 x 10.2 cm)	$3/8$" (9.5 mm)	5	15" (38.1 cm)	6	13" (33 cm)
4" x 6" (10.2 x 15.2 cm)	4" x 6" (10.2 x 15.2 cm)	$1/2$" (1.3 cm)	5	17" (43.2 cm)	6	15" (38.1 cm)
6" x 10" (15.2 x 25.4 cm)	6" x 10" (15.2 x 25.4 cm)	$5/8$" (1.6 cm)	5	25" (63.5 cm)	8	21" (53.3 cm)
8" x 12" (20.3 x 30.5 cm)	8" x 12" (20.3 x 30.5 cm)	$5/8$" (1.6 cm)	7	30" (76.2 cm)	10	26" (66 cm)
10" x 15" (25.4 x 38.1 cm)	10" x 14" (25.4 x 35.6 cm)	$5/8$" (1.6 cm)	9	35" (88.9 cm)	12	31" (78.7 cm)
12" x 18" (30.5 x 45.7 cm)	12" x 14" (30.5 x 35.6 cm)	$3/4$" (1.9 cm)	9	40" (102 cm)	14	34" (86.4 cm)

TWINING	HEIGHT	WEAVERS	LASHING	RIM*
6 1/2' (1.98 m) #1 round	2 1/2" (6.1 cm)	23" (58.4 cm)	6' (1.8 m) of 11/64" (4.4 mm) flat-oval	3/8" (9.5 mm) flat-oval
8' (2.4 m) #2 round	3 1/2" (8.9 cm)	27" (68.6 cm)	7' (2.1 m) of 3/16" (5 mm) flat-oval	3/8" (9.5 mm) flat-oval
12' (3.6 m) #2 round	5" (12.7 cm)	41" (104.1 cm)	9' (2.7 m) of 1/4" (6 mm) flat-oval	1/2" (1.3 cm) flat-oval
15' (4.5 m) #3 round	6" (15.2 cm)	49" (124.5 cm)	11' (3.3 m) of 1/4" (6 mm) flat- oval	1/2" (1.3 cm) flat-oval
19' (5.8 m) #3 round	7" (17.8 cm)	60" (1.5 m)	14' (4.3 m) of 7 mm flat-oval	5/8" (1.6 cm) flat-oval
23' (7 m) #3 round	8" (20.3 cm)	72" (1.8 m)	16' (4.9 m) of 7mm flat-oval	5/8" (1.6 cm) flat-oval

* Your hidden weaver should be a little narrower than the rim material.

Rim filler can be anything that fills the space between the rim pieces.

SHAPING & EMBELLISHMENTS

The next three baskets focus on shaping, and their sides slope instead of going straight up. As a cooking recipe may read, "Add pepper to taste," these baskets also include some optional overlay accents to add a little spice. But if you're in a hurry, skip the overlay. In these projects, you'll use all of the techniques discussed so far, plus you'll learn cross-stitching, curls, and wave-weave.

(Top of page) **SHANNON WEBER**, *Raven Sings (detail)*, 1999. Photo by Rick Hiser

(Directly above) **DONNA SAKAMOTO CRISPIN**, *Cathead Basket*, 1995. 9" x 10½" x 9" (22.9 x 26.7 x 22.9 cm); reed, cane, birch twig. Photo by artist

Sharp Top Basket with Diamonds

Following the slant of the handle called a sharp top D, this basket slopes inward and gets smaller as you work up to the top, each row pulling in the sides a little bit more. You'll also add two colors of dyed reed to the top of the basket to enhance the cross-stitching.

BASIC SKILLS NEEDED

laying out a base, page 19

twining, page 19

upsetting, page 20

start-and-stop plain weave, page 21

adding a rim, page 22

lashing, page 29

TECHNIQUES YOU'LL LEARN

cross-stitching overlay

shaping a sharp top basket

FINISHED SIZE 9 X 9 X 8 INCHES
(22.9 X 22.9 X 20.3 CM),
NOT INCLUDING HANDLE HEIGHT

OTHER SUPPLIES

brown and olive basket dyes

QUANTITY	MATERIAL & DIMENSIONS	LENGTH	FUNCTION
13	³/₄" (1.9 cm) flat reed	30" (76.2 cm)	stakes
1	sharp top D handle 8" x 12" (20.3 x 30.5 cm)		handle
1	#2 round reed	11' (3.3 m)	twining
2	¹/₂" (1.3 cm) flat reed	38" (96.5 cm)	weavers
24	¹/₄" (6 mm) flat-oval reed	38" (96.5 cm)	weavers*
1	³/₈" (9.5 mm) flat reed	32" (81.2 cm)	hidden weaver
2	¹/₂" (1.3 cm) flat-oval reed	32" (81.2 cm)	rim
1	#3 seagrass	32" (81.2 cm)	rim filler
1	5 mm binder cane	8' (2.4 m)	lashing
2	5 mm binder cane	6' (1.8 m)	cross-stitching

*dye 4 pieces brown, 2 pieces olive

INSTRUCTIONS

1 Mark the centers of the thirteen 30-inch (76.2 cm) stakes on the wrong side. Lay out the bottom of the basket, wrong side up, in a plain weave, using seven stakes in one direction and six stakes and the handle in the other. Work the material damp. Center the handle in its side and place it on top of the center stake it crosses (photo 1).

2 Adjust the bottom to 8 x 8 inches (20.3 x 20.3 cm). Square the base and mark the corners so you can correct any later slippage.

3 Use the #2 round reed to twine two rows around the base.

4 Upsett the stakes, using the two pieces of ¹/₂-inch (1.3 cm) flat reed to turn up the sides. Use a start-and-stop weave. All weavers should be right side out.

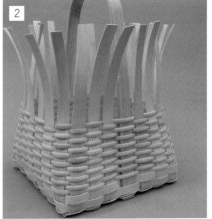

5 The basket's tapered shape (photo 2) can be a bit tricky as it follows the same slant as the handle. Each row must be pulled a little tighter than the row below. Don't pull in the first two rows or the corners will pucker; do pull in

the next 15 rows of undyed, $^1/_4$-inch (6 mm) flat-oval reed. Precutting the weavers to a specific length helps you determine how much the sides are pulling in. You should be cutting a little more off of each weaver as you go up. The exact amount will vary depending on the width of the reed and the exact shape of your basket.

6 As you shape the basket, pulling in as you work up, the stakes will move too close together for the weavers to slip down between them. Taper the stakes (photo 3) so the weavers fit. Use shears to take a little off each side of each stake, gradually reducing their width from $^3/_4$ inch (1.9 cm) to $^1/_2$ inch (1.3 cm). The longer blades of paper shears work better than basket shears. Don't pull in the side too much; a too-small circumference creates a football-shape top rather than a circle. I actually like my tops to be somewhat rectangular (i.e., a bit looser than a circle) because it's easier to get things in and out of the basket.

7 Weave in the dyed $^1/_4$-inch (6 mm) flat-oval reed (photo 4). Notice that two pieces are worked together in each row, one on top of the other in the same over-under pattern, almost as if you've made a mistake. Cross-stitching looks better worked over $^1/_2$-inch-wide (1.3 cm) weavers, but the slope of the sides makes it nearly impossible to add a wide weaver. Pairing two narrower weavers solves the problem and adds an interesting texture.

8 Add three rows of the natural $^1/_4$-inch (6 mm) flat-oval weavers above the dyed weavers to finish the sides.

9 Now you'll add the $^3/_8$-inch (9.5 mm) flat reed hidden weaver. Fold and tuck the outside stakes. Add the rim. Use the 5 mm binder cane to lash and the #3 seagrass as filler. Put an X at the handles (Muffin Basket, page 29). You'll need to soak the cane a bit longer than the reed; its right side is shiny and should face the outside.

10 Cross-stitching adds interesting detail and texture, and is done in two stages using the 5 mm binder cane. Choose the most even, supple piece of cane you can find. Slip one end

under any stake on the outside of the bottom double row of dyed reed, the cane's wrong side facing up and its tail end pointing to the right side of the stake. Fold the long end over that stake (now the right side faces out) and, working to the right, take the cane diagonally up to the next outside stake on the top row of dyed reed. Pass the end right to left and through the space between that stake and the dyed reed, keeping the cane untwisted and flat against the basket wall. When the cane is threaded through, its *wrong* side will face out. Zigzag up and down, around the stakes (photo 5). When you reach the starting stake, pass under it, being careful not to dislodge the beginning of the cane. Clip off the end of the cane so it doesn't show.

11 Repeat step 10 using the second piece of cane, but weave it through the unused spaces between the stakes and dyed reed. It will cross the first row, making diamonds (photo 6). End it as you did the first one.

Williamsburg X's & O's Basket with Curls

Very narrow at the base, this easy-access basket opens out as the sides go up, following the profile of the Williamsburg handle. It has no twining around the base, which makes upsetting a little more challenging because the stakes aren't locked in place. Add an overlay of curls for a final decorative touch.

BASIC SKILLS NEEDED

laying out a base, page 19

upsetting, page 20

start-and-stop plain weave, page 21

adding a rim, page 22

lashing, page 29

OTHER SUPPLIES

dark green and
medium peach basket dye

TECHNIQUES YOU'LL LEARN

adding an overlay of curls

shaping a Williamsburg basket

upsetting without twining

FINISHED SIZE 8^1/$_2$ X 8^1/$_2$ X 5 INCHES
(21.6 X 21.6 X 12.7 CM),
NOT INCLUDING HANDLE HEIGHT

QUANTITY	MATERIAL & DIMENSIONS	LENGTH	FUNCTION
9	$^5/_8$" (1.6 cm) flat reed	23" (58.4 cm)	stakes
1	Williamsburg handle $5^1/_2$" x 9" (14 x 23 cm)		handle
3	$^1/_2$" (1.3 cm) flat reed	34" (86.4 cm)	weavers*
13	$^1/_4$" (6 mm) flat-oval reed	34" (86.4 cm)	weavers**
1	$^3/_8$" (9.5 mm) flat reed	34" (86.4 cm)	hidden weaver
2	$^1/_2$" (1.3 cm) flat-oval reed	34" (86.4 cm)	rim
1	#3 seagrass	34" (86.4 cm)	rim filler
1	$^1/_4$" (6 mm) flat-oval reed	14' (4.3 m)	lashing
2	7 mm flat reed	5' (1.5 m)	curls

*dye 2 pieces dark green   **dye 3 pieces medium peach

INSTRUCTIONS

1 Mark the centers of the nine 23-inch (58.4 cm) stakes on the wrong side. Work the materials damp. Lay out the basket bottom in plain weave, wrong side up. Align five stakes in one direction and four stakes plus the handle in the other. The handle should be in the middle of its set and under the center stake crossing it (photo 1). Center all of the pieces. Adjust the bottom to $5^1/_2$ x $5^1/_2$ inches (14 x 14 cm). Mark the corners.

2 Upsett the basket. Use the $^1/_4$-inch (6 mm) flat-oval reed in a start-and-stop weave to weave the first four rows, right side to the outside. (It's easier to use the narrower reed when weaving around the small base.) The weavers are long enough to go around the basket at its widest point. You'll have to cut quite a lot from the first few rows but less and less as you work up.

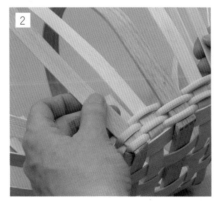

3 Shaping this basket is challenging. Let it flare out as you weave up the sides, or the top will be oval instead of round. The side shape should follow the flare of the handle. After the second row is in place, pull out the stakes to flare the corners (photo 2), and press open the stakes from the inside before you add each row (photo 3). Adding the piece of natural, $^1/_2$-inch (1.3 cm) flat reed above the first four rows also helps force open the stakes.

4 Use the remaining weavers to weave up the sides of the basket, adding the dyed reed in the order shown in photograph 4.

5 Add the hidden weaver (the ³/₈-inch [9.5 mm] flat reed piece), then pack and level the sides. Cut off the inside stakes, and fold and tuck the outside ones. Add the rim and lash it on. Make an X on both sides at the handle and hide the lashing's ends between the layers of the rim (photo 5). You could call it quits at this point, but it's more fun to add the curls.

6 Curls can be worked horizontally, vertically, or diagonally. They are similar to the cross-stitching used in the Sharp Top Basket (page 35), but instead of lying flat against the surface of the basket, the weaver has a twist. That twist can be folded and flattened against the basket wall or left loose for a deeper texture. The weaver used to make curls must be top quality, very flexible, and kept damp; you'll be asking a lot of it and it will tend to crack.

You'll work the first row of curls around the uppermost dyed ¹/₂-inch (1.3 cm) flat weaver. Slip one end of the curl material between an outside stake and the weaver, wrong side up (photo 6). The direction of the twist matters; twist the curl material exactly as shown at right. Cut the end of the weaver into a point (to facilitate threading), then thread it up under the dyed ¹/₂-inch (1.3 cm) flat reed as you pass it over the next stake to the right (photo 7). Twist it again and thread it behind the next outside stake, left to right (photo 8). Twist it again and thread it down behind the dyed ¹/₂-inch (1.3 cm) flat reed. Make another twist; again, go behind the next outside stake. You've now completed one repeat (photo 9). Repeat the

twisting and threading around the basket, then slip the end behind the stake where you started. As you work, adjust the curls as shown.

7 Add a second row of curls around the lower row of dyed ¹/₂-inch (1.3 cm) flat reed, working in a direction opposite to the upper row (photo 10). End where you began.

Trinket Basket

Because this basket has no handle, you can make it any shape you want. It's accented with a Japanese wave-weave crafted from round reed. Calling wave-weave an overlay is a bit of a stretch: it can be added to a completed basket, but it's easier to do as you weave up the sides.

BASIC SKILLS NEEDED

laying out a base, page 19

twining, page 19

upsetting, page 20

start-and-stop plain weave, page 21

adding a rim, page 22

TECHNIQUES YOU'LL LEARN

wave-weave

double-stitched lashing

FINISHED SIZE 6 X 6 X 5 INCHES
(15.2 X 15.2 X 12.7 CM)

OTHER MATERIALS

purple and green basket dye

QUANTITY	MATERIAL & DIMENSIONS	LENGTH	FUNCTION
10	$^5/_8$" (1.6 cm) flat reed	20" (50.8 cm)	stakes
1	#2 round reed	8' (2.4 m)	twining
10	$^1/_4$" (6 mm) flat-oval reed	29" (73.7 cm)	weavers
3	$^1/_2$" (1.3 cm) flat reed	29" (73.7 cm)	weavers*
1	#2 round reed	12' (3.6 m)	wave-weave**
1	$^3/_8$" (9.5 mm) flat reed	29" (73.7 cm)	hidden weaver
2	$^1/_2$" (1.3 cm) flat-oval reed	29" (73.7 cm)	rim
1	#3 seagrass	29" (73.7 cm)	rim filler
1	$^1/_4$" (6 mm) flat-oval reed	9' (2.7 m)	lashing

*dye all purple   **dye all green

INSTRUCTIONS

1 Mark the centers of the ten 20-inch (50.8 cm) stakes on the rough side. Lay out the basket bottom in a plain weave, rough side up, five stakes in each direction. Work materials damp. Center all the pieces. Adjust the bottom to 5 x 5 inches (12.7 x 12.7 cm). Mark the corners.

2 Using the #2 round reed, twine two rows around the base of the basket.

3 Upsett the stakes, using the $^1/_4$-inch (6 mm) flat-oval reed to weave the first three rows, right side to the outside. Use start-and-stop weave and overlap each row by a width of four stakes. Start each row on a side of the basket different from the row below.

4 Gently fold the dyed #2 round reed in half; don't crimp it. Start a $^1/_2$-inch (1.3 cm) flat reed weaver on top of an appropriate stake, and slip the folded loop in place (photo 1).

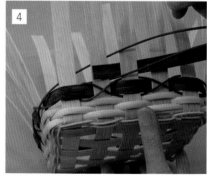

5 Use the round reed to make an X (photo 2). Continue weaving the flat reed into place as the round reed waves over and under it, crossing over the outside stakes.

The round reed X's appear only on the basket exterior. When you complete the row, overlap only the $^1/_2$-inch (1.3 cm) flat reed by two stakes, simply slipping it in place between its beginning point and the outside stake. Don't clip off the round reed.

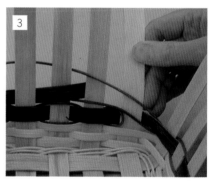

6 Start the next $^1/_2$-inch (1.3 cm) flat reed weaver on the same side of the basket, moving over one

stake and allowing the round reed to skip over two stakes on the inside of the basket (photo 3). Bring the round reed back to the outside of the basket (photo 4). Wave-weave around, again ending with a two-stake overlap.

9 Add the $^3/_8$-inch (9.5 mm) flat reed hidden weaver. Pack the sides and level the top.

10 Clip off the inside stakes and fold and tuck the stakes ending on the outside, then add the rim pieces.

7 The third row also starts on the same side of the basket and ends with a two-stake overlap. It also moves over one stake to start, the round reed skipping over two stakes on the inside. End the round reed inside of the basket, slipping the ends under the third $^1/_2$-inch (1.3 cm) flat reed weaver (photo 5).

11 This basket has a double-stitched rim. Two wraps of lashing are placed into each hole formed by the stakes instead of one (photo 7). End by hiding the ends of the lashing inside the rim.

8 Using start-and-stop weave, weave in the seven remaining $^1/_4$-inch (6 mm) flat-oval weavers, pulling in each row as you work up. Force in the stakes as you weave each row (photo 6). Overlap each row by four stakes, starting each row on a different side of the basket than the previous one.

COLOR

The next three baskets focus on color. Until now, you've used dyed reed as an accent: a little here, a little there. Though the next three baskets are woven in plain weave, the placement of dyed reed makes the baskets look far more complicated than they really are. You'll need all the basic basket skills you've learned up until now.

(Top of page) **BJ CRAWFORD,** *Shifting Arrows*, 2001. 12" x 15" x 6$\frac{1}{2}$" (30.5 x 38.1 x 16.5 cm); space-dyed flat reed, three-rod arrows, French randing. Photo by Blair Logue

(Directly above) **BLAIR J. LOGUE**, *Moon Shadow/Harvest Moon*, 1999. 10" x 10" (25.4 x 25.4 cm) and 8 x 8 (20.3 x 20.3 cm); flat and flat-oval reed, handmade reed handle, ash swing handle. Photo by artist

Simple Square Basket

The Simple Square is the largest basket so far. It has a filled bottom, meaning there are no holes for crumbs to fall through, and it's the first to have a true double lashing. This project utilizes space-dyed reed, which features two or more colors in a repeating pattern on the same piece of reed. Interesting patterns appear on their own, so you don't have to follow color sequences or make design decisions.

BASIC SKILLS NEEDED

laying out a base, page 19

twining, page 19

upsetting, page 20

start-and-stop plain weave, page 21

adding a rim, page 22

lashing, page 23

TECHNIQUES YOU'LL LEARN

space-dyeing reed

filling a bottom

double-crossed lashing

FINISHED SIZE 11 X 11 X 8 INCHES
(27.9 X 27.9 X 20.3 CM), NOT INCLUDING
HANDLE HEIGHT

MATERIALS

See page 46 for list of materials

OTHER SUPPLIES*

rubber bands

cotton string

basket dye in blue, green, and brown, or 3 colors of your choice

3 containers to hold dye baths

*Buy these materials if you wish to space-dye the reed yourself, or you can purchase predyed reed from basket suppliers. You will need to dye about 2 coils of ⅝" (1.6 cm) flat and 2 pieces of ¼" (6 mm) flat-oval, each 11' (3.3 m) long.

INSTRUCTIONS

stakes and eight fillers in the other. The fillers should lie under the center stake (photo 2). Alternate the stakes and fillers, packing them tightly against one another and starting and ending with a stake (photo 3).

1 To space-dye reed, divide the two coils of ⁵/₈-inch (1.6 cm) flat reed into three bundles. Add the ¹/₄-inch (6 mm) flat-oval reed to a bundle (it will serve as lashing later). Use a rubber band to secure one end of each bundle to reduce tangling. Coil the bundles, tying them loosely with cotton string. Soak the reed in water while you use hot water to make up three pots of dye. Set one coil into each container, about one third of the coil in the dye. Let soak. Remove the reed and reheat the dye baths.

Put each coil into a different color dye, rotating the coil to dye another section (photo 1). Repeat the process to dye the final third of each coil. Untie the bundles and let the reed dry, then cut pieces as required for the basket.

2 Mark the centers of all the stakes and fillers on the wrong side. Work materials damp.

3 Lay out the bottom of the basket in a plain weave: nine stakes in one direction and nine

4 Adjust the bottom to 10 x 10 inches (25.4 x 25.4 cm). Square it up and mark the corners.

5 Before you fold and tuck the fillers, it's helpful to trim them.

MATERIALS			
QUANTITY	**MATERIAL & DIMENSIONS**	**LENGTH**	**FUNCTION**
18	space-dyed ⁵/₈" (1.6 cm) flat reed*	34" (86.4 cm)	stakes
8	³/₈" (9.5 mm) flat reed, undyed	16" (40.6 cm)	fillers
1	#3 round reed	8' (2.4 m)	twining
10	space-dyed ⁵/₈" (1.6 cm) flat reed*	46" (66.8 cm)	weavers
1	¹/₂" (1.3 cm) flat reed	46" (116.8 cm)	hidden weaver
1	square notched U handle 10" (25.4 cm)		handle
2	⁵/₈" (1.6 cm) flat-oval reed	46" (116.8 cm)	rim
1	#3 seagrass	46" (116.8 cm)	rim filler
2	space-dyed ¹/₄" (6 mm) flat-oval reed	11' (3.3 m)	lashing

Fold them against the base to gauge how much to trim, then trim them. Fold the fillers around the outside stakes and tuck them in pairs under the adjacent stake (photo 4). See the little V's formed by the fillers? They're called *crow's feet*.

6 Starting on a side without the crow's feet, twine once around the base. I like to start on the third stake from the corner.

7 Fold and crimp the stakes at the edge of the basket base. Upsett the stakes, using the space-dyed ⁵/₈-inch (1.6 cm) flat reed in a plain weave up the sides of the basket. With the right side of the weavers to the outside, use a start-and-stop weave and work the sides straight up (photo 5). Since the basket size is determined by the handle width, use the handle as a size gauge.

8 Use the hidden weaver to weave the top row of the basket. Pack the sides and make everything even. Fold and tuck the stakes.

9 Insert the handle. It can go in either direction because the basket is square; I prefer putting it on the sides without the crow's feet. Taper the end of the handle to a point so it won't show on the outside of the basket, and sand it until it's smooth. Locate the stake at the center of the side wall and slip the end of the handle behind a lower weaver, parallel to the stake (which weaver depends on the handle length). Push down the handle to position the notch at the bottom edge of the hidden weaver (photo 6).

10 Fit the rim and use the seagrass as filler. The lashing on this basket incorporates two pieces of lashing instead of one. The second crosses the first, so you won't need to make an X at the handle. Simply start with one piece and lash, ignoring the handle (photo 7). Hide its ends.

11 Now use the second piece of lashing to lash the rim, slanting it in the opposite direction (photo 8). Be sure to start on the opposite side of the basket so the lashing ends at a point different from the first piece.

Square-to-Round Storage Basket

This basket is a simple shape but it uses the placement of dyed and natural reed to great effect. By alternating light and dark stakes around the basket, interesting color patterns build up the sides. There's no end to the patterns you can weave by changing weaver sizes and colors. Many traditional Cherokee baskets are made using this method. The colors shown are dark green and rust.

BASIC SKILLS NEEDED

laying out a base with fillers, page 46

twining, page 19

upsetting, page 20

start-and-stop plain weave, page 21

adding a rim, page 22

lashing, page 23

OTHER MATERIALS

dark green and rust basket dye

TECHNIQUES YOU'LL LEARN

building patterns by crossing different colors

FINISHED SIZE 10^1/$_2$ X 10^1/$_2$ X 7 INCHES (26.7 X 26.7 X 17.8 CM)

MATERIALS

QUANTITY	MATERIAL & DIMENSIONS	LENGTH	COLOR	FUNCTION
14	^{3}/$_4$" (1.9 cm) flat reed	28" (71.1 cm)	7 natural, 7 dyed dark green	stakes
6	^{3}/$_8$" (9.5 mm) flat reed	14" (35.6 cm)	all dyed rust	filler strips
1	#2 round reed	14' (4.3 m)	natural	twining
5	^{1}/$_2$" (1.3 cm) flat reed	41" (104.1 cm)	natural	weavers
3	^{1}/$_2$" (1.3 cm) flat reed	41" (104.1 cm)	all dyed rust	weavers
9	^{3}/$_{16}$" (5 mm) flat reed	41" (104.1 cm)	5 dyed dark green, 4 rust	weavers
1	^{3}/$_8$" (9.5 mm) flat reed	41" (104.1 cm)	natural	hidden weaver
2	^{1}/$_2$" (1.3 cm) flat-oval reed	41" (104.1 cm)	natural	rim
1	#6 round reed	41" (104.1 cm)	natural	rim filler
1	^{3}/$_{16}$" (5 mm) flat-oval reed	8' (2.4 m)	natural	lashing

INSTRUCTIONS

1 Mark the centers of the fourteen 28-inch (71.1 cm) stakes and six filler strips, on their wrong sides. Soak them until pliable. The wrong side of the reed should face the inside of the basket.

2 Lay out the basket bottom in a plain weave, alternating dyed and natural stakes. Orient seven stakes in one direction, starting and ending with dark stakes, and seven stakes and six filler strips in the other direction, starting and ending with natural stakes. Alternate fillers and stakes, and pack tightly against them. The central natural stake should cross over the central dyed stake (photo 1). Position the filler strips on top of the central natural stake. Center everything. Adjust and square the base to 8 x 8 inches (20.3 x 20.3 cm) (photo 2). Mark the corners.

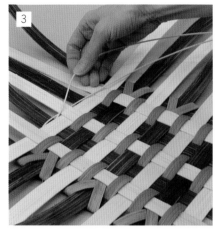

3 Fold the filler strips around the outside stakes and tuck them in pairs under the next stake.

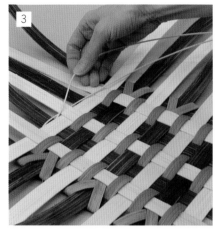

4 Starting on a side without fillers, use the #2 round reed to twine two rows around the bottom (photo 3).

5 Fold and crimp the stakes at the edge of the basket base. Upsett them, using the 1/2-inch (1.3 cm) and 3/16-inch (5 mm) flat reed in start-and-stop weave to weave up the sides. Working straight up, add weavers to the basket sides, as shown in photo 4, or in any order you choose.

6 Use the 3/8-inch (9.5 mm) flat reed to weave the top row of the basket. Adjust the sides, pack down the weavers, and make everything even.

7 Fold and tuck the stakes.

8 Use the two pieces of 1/2-inch (1.3 cm) flat-oval reed to form the rim.

9 Use the #6 round reed to fill the gap between the two pieces of flat-oval reed, running it around the top edge of the basket and ending on the side with the rim overlaps. Don't fit it too closely yet; wait until the lashing is mostly done.

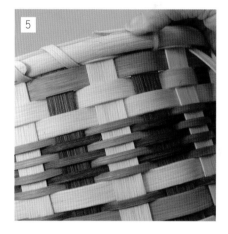

10 Lash the rim. At the point where the ends of round reed meet, cut the ends in a bevel (photo 5). Use lashing to hold them in place and cover the join.

11 Hide the lashing ends between the layers of the rim.

Shadow-Weave Rectangular Basket

Named after the fabric design called shadow weave, this basket has light and dark stakes that alternate and cross, and build up to create interesting designs. The basket is created from a very simple plain weave; be sure to follow the exact sequence of colors and sizes or your basket won't look the same. This design also features side handles and decorative, diagonal filler strips.

BASIC SKILLS NEEDED	TECHNIQUES YOU'LL LEARN	OTHER SUPPLIES
laying out a base, page 19	adding side handles	blue basket dye
twining, page 19	creating more color play	white craft glue
upsetting, page 20	adding diagonal filler strips	
start-and-stop plain weave, page 21		
adding a rim, page 22	FINISHED SIZE 10 X 13 X 6 INCHES	
lashing, page 29	(25.4 X 33 X 15.2 CM)	

QUANTITY	MATERIAL & DIMENSIONS	LENGTH	COLOR	FUNCTION
9	$^5/_8$" (1.6 cm) flat reed	25" (63.5 cm)	4 dyed blue, 5 natural	stakes
7	$^5/_8$" (1.6 cm) flat reed	28" (71.1 cm)	2 dyed blue, 5 natural	stakes
1	$^3/_8$" (9.5 mm) flat reed	9' (2.7 m)*	natural	filler strips
1	#2 round reed	8' (2.4 m)	natural	twining
7	$^1/_2$" (1.3 cm) flat reed	44" (111.8 cm)	3 dyed blue, 4 natural	weavers
6	$^1/_4$" (6 mm) flat reed	44" (111.8 cm)	4 dyed blue, 2 natural	weavers
1	$^3/_8$" (9.5 mm) flat reed	44" (111.8 cm)	natural	hidden weaver
2	3" (7.6 cm) side handles			handles
2	$^1/_2$" (1.3 cm) flat-oval reed	44" (111.8 cm)	natural	rim
1	#3 seagrass	44" (111.8 cm)	natural	rim filler
1	$^1/_4$" (6 mm) flat-oval reed	8' (2.4 m)	natural	lashing

*you'll cut exact lengths as you weave the filler into the base

INSTRUCTIONS

1 Mark the centers of the nine 25-inch (63.5 cm) and seven 28-inch (71.1 cm) stakes on the wrong sides. The rough side of the reed should face the inside of the basket.

2 Lay out the bottom of the basket in a simple plain weave. Work materials damp. Place the dyed and natural stakes, as shown in photograph 1, orienting the 25-inch (63.5 cm) stakes in one direction and the 28-inch (71.1 cm) stakes in the other. Make sure the central 28-inch stake lies *under* the center 25-inch stake. Center everything, adjusting and squaring the base to 8 x 10 inches (20.3 x 25.4 cm). Because the filler strips will be woven diagonally across the base, pulling things out of alignment, be sure to mark the corners so the base can be returned to its proper size.

3 Soak the filler strips. Weave them diagonally across the base, cutting them to length as you weave them in. Cut the ends into points and hide them between the stake crossings (photo 2). Square up the base, making sure it's 8 x 10 inches (20.3 x 25.4 cm). Carefully add a drop of white glue at both ends of each filler strip to hold it in place. Weight the base and let the glue dry.

4 Use the #2 round reed to twine one row around the bottom.

5 Fold and crimp the stakes at the edge of the basket base.

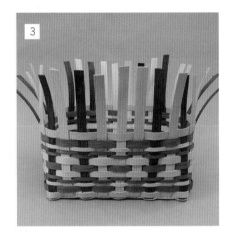

6 Upsett the stakes, using the $^1/_2$-inch (1.3 cm) and $^1/_4$-inch (6 mm) flat reed in a start-and-stop weave. Work straight up the sides of the basket. Follow the order shown in photograph 3, or weave up the sides in any order you choose.

7 Use the $^3/_8$-inch (9.5 mm) flat reed to weave the top row of the basket. Adjust the sides, pack down the weavers, and make everything even.

8 Fold and tuck the outside stakes to the inside and clip off the inside stakes.

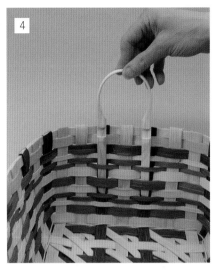

9 Place the side handles on the 8-inch (20.3 cm) ends of the basket. Work them down between the weavers and the stakes in the side wall of the basket (photo 4). Push in the handle until the notches line up with the hidden weaver. The depth of insertion, exactly which weavers you go behind, and how far down the handle ends extend will depend on the handle length.

10 Use the two pieces of $^1/_2$-inch (1.3 cm) flat-oval reed to form the rim.

11 Using the #3 seagrass, fill the gap between the two pieces of flat-oval reed (photo 5).

12 Lash the rim, starting on the long side opposite the rim overlaps. When you reach the handles, make an X at each side of each handle (photo 6).

13 Finish the lashing by hiding the ends between the layers of the rim.

HANGING BASKETS

The next two baskets hang on the wall. The first is a small wall basket with beaded ornamentation and the second is a garlic basket. They're useful around the house and make great gifts, too.

(Top of page) **HELEN SCHWARTZ**, *Summer Wall Basket*, 2002. 10" x 4" x 4" (25.4 x 10.2 x 10.2 cm); reed, wooden beads. Photo by artist

(Directly above) **BJ CRAWFORD**, *Letter Basket* (detail), 2003. 6" x 1" x 6" (15.2 x 2.5 x 15.2 cm); flat reed, hemp twine, wooden beads. Photo by Evan Bracken

Letter Basket

This little, flat basket is just the right size to hang by your kitchen door to collect outgoing mail. It can be woven with any sizes or colors of reed and, because it's small, it's a great way to use up leftover pieces. I picked out the bead ornamentation first, then chose dyed reed from my never-ending stash to match. I added some hemp twine for a textural accent, but more round reed would be fun, too.

BASIC SKILLS NEEDED

laying out a base, page 19

twining, page 19

upsetting, page 20

start-and-stop plain weave, page 21

adding a rim, page 22

lashing, page 24

TECHNIQUES YOU'LL LEARN

adding tassel and bead embellishment

FINISHED SIZE 6 X 1 X 6 INCHES (15.2 X 2.5 X 15.2 CM) NOT INCLUDING HANDLE HEIGHT

OTHER SUPPLIES

#16 tapestry needle

hemp twine

assorted 12 mm and 14 mm beads of your choice

INSTRUCTIONS

1 Lightly mark the centers of the five 19-inch (48.3 cm) stakes and the 25-inch (63.5 cm) stake on their right (smooth) sides. Mark the two 24-inch (61 cm) stakes 9½ inches (24.1 cm) from one end. The extra 5 inches (12.7 cm) on these two stakes will extend out from the same side of the base to form the handle.

2 Work with the right side of the reed facing up so it's properly oriented when you start twining up the sides; the rough side should end up inside the basket. Work everything damp, including the hemp, and when working with the hemp, use a doubled strand.

3 Because only one 25-inch (63.5 cm) stake crosses the other seven stakes, the base needs extra help to stay together until you get the first row of twining in place. You can use a spoke weight to hold things down until the twining is started, but my preferred method is to use scraps of narrow reed to weave in four extra rows of weaving, which hold the

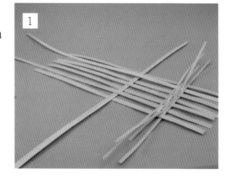

stakes in place. Exact placement isn't necessary; remove the extra rows after completing the first section of twining. Arrange the base pieces, as shown in photograph 1. The 24-inch (61 cm) stakes will form the handle and must protrude from the same side in the #2 and #6 positions. Evenly line up all the stake ends at one end, matching the marks. Adjust their width to 6¼ inches (15.8 cm), keeping their center points in alignment, and weave the 25-inch (63.5 cm) stake (right side up) across. The cross-stake should cross over the top of both outside stakes. Lightly mark the outside edges of the base.

4 Crimp a piece of the #2 round reed not quite in half and slip the fold over an outside stake on the side with the protruding handle pieces. Twine across the stakes, being careful not to shift their positions. Turn the corner, keeping the twining tight. Remove the scrap pieces of weaving and complete the first round of twining. The base should now look like photograph 2.

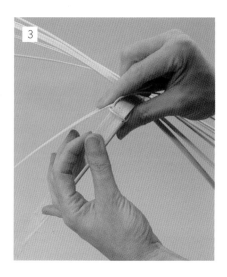

5 Pick up the base and fold the stakes down and away from you (photo 3). Flip down the basket base. The stakes' right side should be on the outside.

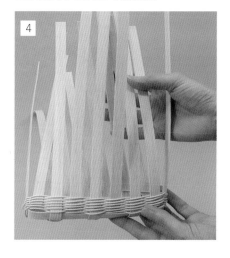

6 Twine four or five rows around the stakes, forcing them to stand upright (photo 4). Add more #2 round reed, if needed (page 13).

7 Using weavers in any colors or size variations desired, use start-and-stop weave to weave up the sides of the basket. For this basket, I chose colors to go with my kitchen: soft blues, roses, yellow, olive, and rust. Avoid overlapping around corners and don't pull in the sides too tightly or oversize greeting cards won't fit in the

basket. Occasionally add a few rows of hemp twining for visual interest. To end the hemp, tie the ends together inside the basket (photo 5) and clip off the tails.

8 Add the 3/8-inch (9.5 mm) flat reed hidden weaver. Clip off the inside stakes but not the handle stakes, even if they end up inside the hidden weaver. Fold and tuck the outside stakes to the inside.

9 To form the handle, bend one of the 24-inch (61 cm) stakes across the back side of the basket and down along the other 24-inch stake. Lap the second stake over the first (photo 6).

10 Use the 1/2-inch (1.3 cm) flat reed to form the rim (flat-oval is too thick and heavy). Place the rim overlaps on the back of the basket inside the handle loop. Thread one end of the hemp onto the tapestry needle and lash the rim with a double strand of hemp twine. Make X's at the handles (page 29). To end the lashing, tie the ends together at the bottom inside edge of the rim and thread them up between the rim's layers.

11 Use an overhand knot to tie some strands of hemp to the sides of the basket (photo 7). Thread the beads onto the twine and secure them with a knot. Your basket is ready to hang!

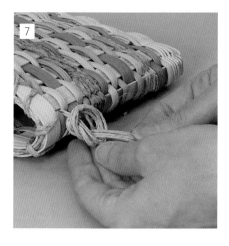

Garlic Basket

This is my version of an old-time favorite that takes only about an hour to make. Fill it to the brim with fresh garlic for a perfect housewarming gift. Use your best-quality ¹/₄-inch (6 mm) flat-oval reed for the braided rim, which you'll learn how to make in this project.

BASIC SKILLS NEEDED

laying out a base, page 19

twining, page 19

TECHNIQUES YOU'LL LEARN

braiding a rim

FINISHED SIZE 4 X 4 X 5 INCHES
(10.2 X 10.2 X 12.7 CM)

OTHER SUPPLIES

white craft glue

MATERIALS			
QUANTITY	MATERIAL & DIMENSIONS	LENGTH	FUNCTION
6	¹/₄" (6 mm) flat-oval reed	25" (63.5 cm)	stakes
	#2 round reed	27' (8.2 m)*	twining
1	#2 round reed	24" (61 cm) long	hanging ring

* will be in several pieces

INSTRUCTIONS

1 Mark the centers of the stakes on the wrong sides. Weave the bottom of the basket in a plain weave, three stakes in each direction. Adjust the base to 1¹/₂ x 1¹/₂ inches (3.8 x 3.8 cm) and mark the corners.

2 Turn over the base, making sure the rounded sides of the stakes face up, so you can start twining on the outside of the base. Wet a piece of the #2 round reed, then crimp and fold it not quite in half. This prevents the two ends from finishing at the same stake, and you won't have to add round reed at the same place.

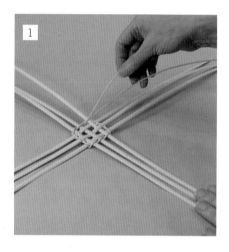

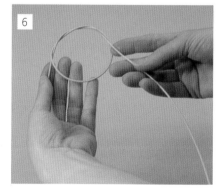

3 Twine once around the base (photo 1).

4 Gently bend up the stakes, cupping them in your hand (photo 2). The base of this basket isn't flat, so don't crimp the stakes at the edge of the twining. Continue twining around, pulling the corner stakes toward each other (photo 3). Space out the stakes evenly; it may take several rounds of twining to get them where you want them.

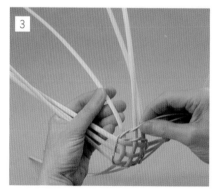

5 Don't tightly pack the rows of twining; space between them allows garlic to "breathe." It's not even necessary to evenly space the rows. I let them wander up and down in interesting patterns (photo 4).

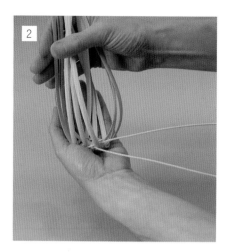

6 If you run out of round reed, simply end it (and immediately begin again) behind a stake (photo 5).

7 Start building one side of the basket taller than the other by spacing the twining farther apart on that side. At this point of the process, the basket I made for this project was 2 inches (5 cm) on one side and 3¹/₂ inches (8.9 cm) on the other; yours may be different. The opening at the top of the basket should be no more than 3¹/₂ inches across. Before adding the hanging ring, pack the next two rows of twining tightly against each other.

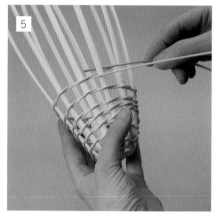

8 To make the hanging ring, start with a 24-inch (61 cm) piece of #2 round reed. Form a loop that's 2¹/₂ inches (6.4 cm) across at one end. Twist the other end through the loop, working around and around to form a ring (photo 6, page 58). I like to wrap for three full circles. Clip off the ends of the reed and use a drop of glue to keep the ends in place.

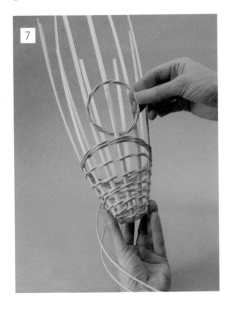

9 Slip the ring around the center stake on the high side of the basket (photo 7).

10 Twine two more rows, packing them tightly against the last two and twining four tightly packed rows in all. End the round reed behind successive stakes, clipping the reed so it lies behind stakes on the back (high side) of the basket. You should have at least 9 inches (22.9 cm) of exposed stake for braiding the rim; push down the twining if necessary.

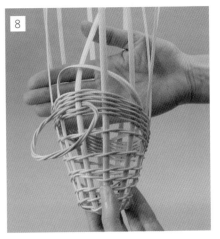

11 Braiding a rim can be confusing at first, but once you understand the process, it's a fast and simple way to finish a basket. Make sure the stakes are well soaked. Start at the back of the basket at the high point where you added the hanging ring. Bend a stake gently to the right and weave it over the next stake to the right, under the next, over the next, and then to the inside of the basket (photo 8). All the while, make sure the rounded side stays to the outside. Don't fold down the stakes too tightly against the twining. You need to leave enough room for the final stakes to be woven in when you end the braid.

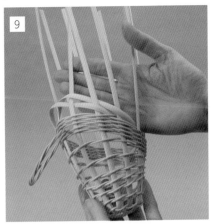

12 Repeat the same process with the next stake to the right and so on, around the circle.

Over, under, over, and in, rounded side always out (photo 9).

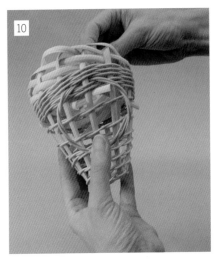

13 Eventually you'll have to thread the stakes into their proper places because the earlier stakes are already bent over (photo 10).

14 When all the stakes are in place, tighten or loosen them to adjust the rim, but wet the rim well beforehand. Once the basket is dry, clip the stakes inside the rim, leaving them long enough so they won't pop out of place.

ROUND BASES

The next three baskets have radial stakes, which allow the bases to be constructed differently from the ones you've done so far. Instead of crossing in a weave structure to form a rectangle, they radiate out from a central point, like the spokes of a wheel. This structure allows you to form a round base for your basket. The next three baskets are woven in spiral weaves: twining, chase, and continuous.

(Top of page) **SHANNON WEBER,** *Little Indian #2,* 1999. 19" x 17" (48.3 x 43.2 cm); rattan, cane, blackberry and black walnut dyes, turquoise, brass beads. Photo by Rick Hiser

(Directly above) **LINDA ARTER SURA,** *Black & White,* 2001. 10" x 8" (25.4 x 20.3 cm); dyed and natural reed. Photo by artist

Cachepot

This cachepot is meant to hold a small potted plant, so it contains a plastic liner that also serves as a guide for shaping the basket itself.

BASIC SKILLS NEEDED

chase-weave, page 12

twining, page 19

start-and-stop plain weave, page 21

TECHNIQUES YOU'LL LEARN

laying out a radial base

folding a no-lash rim

FINISHED SIZE 5^1/$_2$ X 3^1/$_2$ INCHES
(14 X 8.9 CM)

OTHER SUPPLIES

8" x 8" (20.3 x 20.3 cm) pine board with ^{1}/$_{16}$" (1.6 mm) hole drilled in center*

T-pin

cork

small plastic container about 4^1/$_2$" (11.4 cm) across and 3" (7.6 cm) high**

*A piece of cardboard covered with plastic will suffice for one-time use.

**You can also make the basket a little wider to accommodate a wider container, or cut down a taller container to fit. See step 4, page 62.

MATERIALS

QUANTITY	MATERIAL & DIMENSIONS	LENGTH	FUNCTION
8	^{3}/$_8$" (9.5 mm) flat reed	24" (61 cm)	stakes
1	#3 round reed	6' (1.8 m)	base weaver
1	#0 seagrass	34' (10.4 m)	weaver
2	^{1}/$_4$" (6 mm) flat-oval reed	22" (55.9 cm)	weavers
1	^{1}/$_2$" (1.3 cm) flat reed	22" (55.9 cm)	weaver
1	^{1}/$_2$" (1.3 cm) flat reed	22" (55.9 cm)	rim

INSTRUCTIONS

1 To lay out a radial base, some people first stack the pieces, then fan them into a circle. I like to lay them out in crossed pairs. Either way, it's important to have a system to hold them in place. Lay a spoke weight on them or pin them to a board. I use a pine work board with a T-pin sticking up through a small hole drilled through the center. I then push the stakes down on the pin and put a cork on the end of the pin to protect my hands while working.

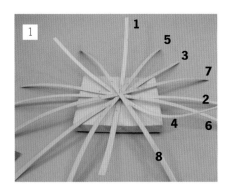

2 Mark the centers of the eight stakes on the wrong sides, then put a mark 1³/₄ inches (4.4 cm) on either side of center. Work all materials damp, including the seagrass. Lay out the stakes (as numbered in photo 1), with center marks at the center of the base and the reed facing wrong side up. Make sure the outer marks form a circle and the stakes are centered.

3 Locate the bottom stake. Clip an end off at an angle to mark it as the beginning stake (you can mark either end).

4 Crimp the piece of #3 round reed in half. Slip the fold over the beginning stake and down to the outside mark. Start your twining at the 1³/₄-inch (4.4 cm) marks, using them as a guide (photo 2). Chase-weave twice around the circle. The width of the finished base should be the same as the plastic liner. If the liner is larger, add a few more rounds to

the base. Remember, chase-weaving differs from twining in that there is no twist between the stakes; the two weavers follow each other around, alternating over and under. After completing the base, clip off the weavers so they lay neatly against the beginning stake and the stake just to its right.

5 Remove the base from the work board and gently bend the stakes upright into a smooth curve, the right side of the reed facing out.

6 Fold the seagrass in half and place the fold over the beginning stake. Twine around the stakes, manipulating the stakes so they stand up as you weave. Use the plastic liner as a guide for shaping; occasionally insert it into the basket to make sure it slips in and out easily (photo 3). As you work up the sides, avoid pulling in too much. The stakes need to be ³/₈ inch (9.5 mm) apart for the folded rim to work.

7 After 10 rounds, or when the basket is 1¹/₄ inches (3.2 cm) deep, stop twining at the beginning stake. Leave the seagrass on the

inside of the basket; don't cut it off. Now use the ¹/₄-inch (6 mm) flat-oval and ¹/₂-inch (1.3 cm) flat reed to add three rows of start-and-stop plain weave.

8 Bring the seagrass back through to the outside of the basket, crossing it behind the last three weavers (photos 4 [outside view] and 5 [inside view]). Twine four more rounds, ending at the beginning stake by clipping off the weavers behind the stakes. Pack the sides and level the top edge.

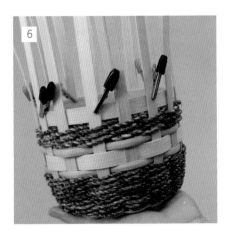

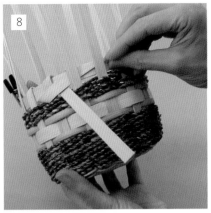

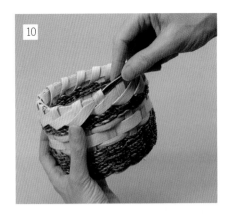

9 The folded no-lash rim construction technique is useful for small baskets, though not strong enough for big ones. Soak the stakes and keep them damp through the entire process. Clip a piece of 1/2-inch (1.3 cm) flat reed to the inside of all the stakes, leaving a 1/4-inch (6 mm) gap above the seagrass (photo 6). Overlap the ends of the 1/2-inch reed about 2 inches (5 cm).

11 Fold the leftmost stake over to the right. Trim it off at an angle to match the top rim. Slip it behind the next upright stake to the right (photo 8).

13 Continue folding, clipping, and wrapping until all stakes are in place. The ending can be a bit confusing because you'll slip the stakes behind stakes that are already folded over. Use a fid or awl to open up the spaces and slip in the ends (photo 10).

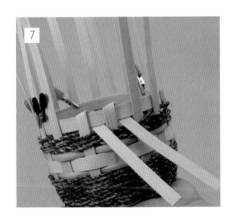

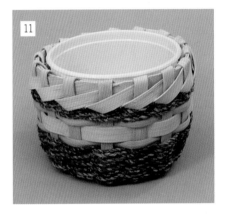

10 Starting anywhere in the circle, fold two adjacent stakes to the inside and around the 1/2-inch (1.3 cm) flat reed, and thread them through to the outside of the basket (photo 7).

12 Now fold the next upright stake (which you slipped the folded stake behind in step 11) to the inside of the basket, around the rim, and back to the outside (photo 9). Once again, two stakes should point down while all others point up.

14 Is the basket's bottom not flat? That often happens with this design. Dampen the entire basket and push up on the bottom so it pokes in instead of out, then weight the top edge of the basket while it dries. Afterward, slip the plastic liner inside (photo 11) and add your potted plant!

Easter Basket

Woven in purple and natural reed, this basket is perfect for Easter and also makes a lovely basket for the flower girl in a wedding.

BASIC SKILLS NEEDED

laying out a radial base, page 62

upsetting, page 20

adding a rim, page 22

lashing, page 29

TECHNIQUES YOU'LL LEARN

using flat-oval weavers to chase-weave

FINISHED SIZE 6^1/$_2$ X 5^1/$_2$ INCHES
(16.5 X 14 CM),
NOT INCLUDING THE HANDLE

OTHER SUPPLIES

purple basket dye

QUANTITY	MATERIAL & DIMENSIONS	LENGTH	FUNCTION
8	$^1/_2$" (1.3 cm) flat reed	22" (56 cm)	stakes*
	#3 round reed	22' (6.7 m)	base weavers**
	$^1/_4$" (6 mm) flat-oval reed	20' (6.1 m)	natural weavers**
	$^1/_4$" (6 mm) flat-oval reed	20' (6.1 m)	dyed weavers***
	6" (15.2 cm)notched U handle		handle
1	$^3/_8$" (9.5 mm) flat reed	28" (71.1 cm)	hidden weaver
2	$^1/_2$" (1.3 cm) flat-oval reed	28" (71.1 cm)	rim
1	#3 seagrass	28" (71.1 cm)	rim filler
1	$^1/_4$" (6 mm) flat-oval reed	5' (1.5 m)	lashing

*dye 4 dark purple   **these weavers can be in several pieces   ***dye all medium purple

INSTRUCTIONS

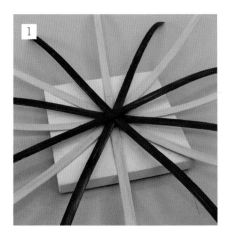

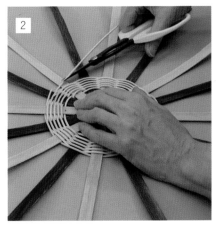

the base is $5^1/_2$ inches [14 cm] across). Add more weavers, if necessary, trying not to add any on the final round. When the base is complete, clip off the weavers (photo 2).

1 This basket's base is similar to the cachepot's, but half the stakes are dyed and alternate with natural stakes to create the pattern. Soak all the stakes. Mark all the centers on the wrong sides and put marks $1^7/_8$ inches (4.8 cm) on either side of the centers. Lay out the damp stakes, wrong side up (photo 1). Place all the natural stakes, then position the dyed ones in-between. Make sure the stakes are centered and the $1^7/_8$-inch (4.8 cm) marks form a circle.

2 Mark the starting stake (on the bottom of the stack) by clipping it off at an angle. Soak a piece of #3 round reed, then use pliers to crimp the fold point so it bends without cracking. Fold it not quite in half, leaving one end a little longer than the other; that way you won't add new weavers at the same stake. Put the folded end around the starting stake and slip it down to the outside circle mark. Using those circle marks as a starting guide, chase-weave five rounds around the base (or until

3 Gently bend up the stakes in a soft curve, right side facing outside (photo 3).

4 Now you'll use two $^1/_4$-inch (6 mm) flat-oval reed weavers (keep them damp) to chase-weave the basket. Use one dyed piece and one natural. I chose a violet color

that's lighter than the stake color for the weavers in the basket shown. First, use paper scissors to slim down an end of each weaver for a length of about 2 feet (61 cm), gently tapering it to a point.

5 Start the weavers at the beginning stake (photo 4). Position the natural weaver to the outside of the natural stakes and the dyed one to the outside of the dyed stakes. The weavers' rounded sides must face out.

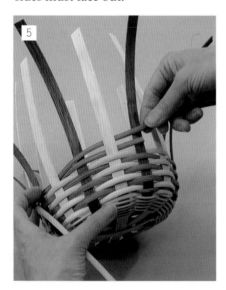

6 Chase-weave in a spiral up the sides of the basket, using the handle as a sizing guide. If the basket isn't the right width, the handle won't fit properly. Add new weavers as needed (photo 5).

7 When the basket is about 5 inches (12.7 cm) high, end the weavers directly above their starting points. Taper them so the top edge is even (photo 6).

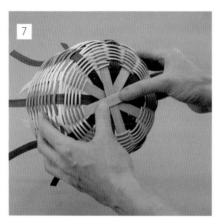

8 If the basket bottom isn't flat, use your thumbs to push it gently (photo 7).

9 Now you'll add a lashed rim to the basket. Why not a folded rim? You can't put on a handle with that type of rim, and what's an Easter basket without a handle? First, weave in the 3/8-inch (9.5 mm) flat reed hidden weaver. Clip off the stakes ending inside the hidden weaver. Fold and tuck the outside stakes to the inside.

10 Add the handle, tapering its ends if necessary and sliding it down along natural stakes, dividing the rim in half. (The handle will be less noticeable from the outside of the basket if it's positioned against natural stakes.)

11 Add the 1/2-inch (1.3 cm) flat-oval reed rim pieces and the seagrass filler, using the 1/4-inch (6 mm) flat-oval reed to lash them in place and putting X's at the handle. Hide the ends.

Spiral Twill Basket

Based on the famed Nantucket Lightship baskets, this cane basket has a slotted wooden base. But that's where the similarity ends. You won't work over a mold, the stakes are flat reed, and the rim and swing handle are attached differently. The basket has an even number of stakes so the handle can be centered on the rim. Since you'll be using a single weaver in a continuous plain weave over an even number of stakes, you'll have to make a "mistake," skipping over two stakes, once each time around. This creates a lazy twill spiral swirl up the side. But as I always tell my students, any mistake repeated three times becomes a design element!

BASIC SKILLS NEEDED
adding a rim, page 22
adding a lock handle, page 52
lashing, page 52

TECHNIQUES YOU'LL LEARN
using a slotted (Nantucket) base
weaving a twill spiral

FINISHED SIZE 8 X 8 X 7 INCHES
(20.3 X 20.3 X 17.8 CM), NOT INCLUDING
THE HANDLE

QUANTITY		MATERIAL & DIMENSIONS	LENGTH	FUNCTION
28		1/2" (1.3 cm) flat reed	11" (27.9 cm)	stakes
1		4" (10.2 cm) wooden Nantucket basket base		base
		#5 binder cane	85' (25.9 m)	weavers (many pieces)
1		8" (20.3 cm) notched wooden swing handle		handle
1		3/8" (9.5 mm) flat reed	29" (73.7 cm)	hidden weaver
2		1/2" (1.3 cm) flat-oval reed	29" (73.7 cm)	rim
1		#3 seagrass	29" (73.7 cm)	rim filler
1		#5 binder cane	8' (2.4 m)	lashing

OTHER SUPPLIES

extra-tacky white craft glue

INSTRUCTIONS

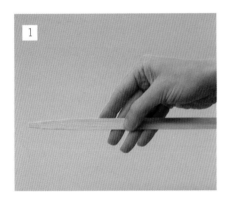

1 Starting 2 inches (5 cm) from the end, taper one end of each stake to 3/16 inches (5 mm) wide (photo 1). Putting a drop of glue on each tapered end, slip all 28 stakes (tapered sides in, right sides up) into the slot in the base. Evenly distribute the stakes around the base and let them dry. Work the stakes and weavers right sides up.

2 Use paper shears to thin the width of a piece of #5 binder cane lengthwise for about 9 feet (2.7 m), tapering it to a point.

3 Dampen the stakes and weaver. Start weaving anywhere in the circle, marking the starting stake by clipping off the end at an angle to make it easy to find. Slip the end of the weaver into the slot and bend it over to start a plain weave around the stakes, keeping the cane's glossy side face up. Pack the weaver as tightly as possible; if the weaver slips into the slot, it will help hold the stakes in place.

4 If you continue weaving over one/under one as you start into the second round, the weaver will match the row below instead of alternating with it because there's an even number of stakes. Simply skip once over two stakes (photo 2). Now return to plain weave around the base, the weave alternating

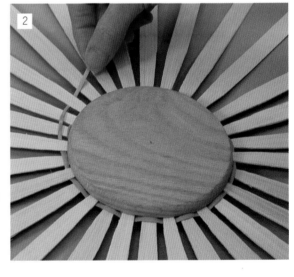

with the row below. When the weave meets the first skip, skip two stakes again, then plain weave the rest of the round. The little twill skip advances by one stake each round, spiraling around the basket (photos 3 and 4, page 69).

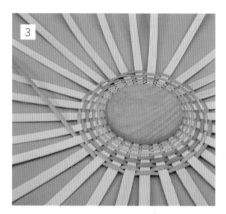

5 Weave the base flat until it measures 7 inches (17.8 cm) across. Add new weavers as needed (page 13), but avoid splicing in new weavers at the twill skips.

6 Dampen the stakes and bend them up in a gentle curve (photo 4). Weave up the sides, using the handle as a width guide, until the basket is 6¹/₂ inches (16.5 cm) tall. Pack the sides well as you go. After achieving the desired height, do one final packing; you may still need to add a few more rows.

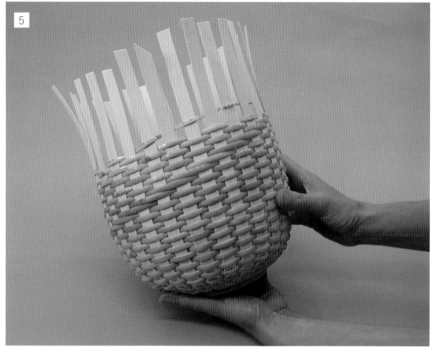

7 Taper the end of the weaver, ending it above the starting point (photo 5).

8 Add the hidden weaver in a start-and-stop plain weave, overlapping four stakes. Start it just to the right of the final skip in the row below so it alternates with that row for most of the circumference.

9 Clip off the stakes, ending on the inside of the hidden weaver. Fold and tuck the outside stakes inside.

10 Add the handle, taking the spiral into consideration and evenly dividing the stakes.

11 Clip the rim pieces in place and lash with the binder cane, putting X's at the handle. Because Nantucket bases eliminate the bulky bottoms of radial bases, the basket should sit flat with no extra shaping.

NEW WEAVES

The next four baskets feature three different weave structures. The Cat-Head Bowl is woven in a 2-1 twill and the Short Cuts Basket has an area of French randing set off by triple weave. The Bathroom Catch-Alls have areas of 2-2 twill set off by triple weave. By reversing the twill, you'll create an entirely different look for Catch-All number two!

(Top of page) **BLAIR J. LOGUE**, *Blair's Square*, 1999. 10" x 10" (25.4 x 25.4 cm); flat reed, ash handle. Photo by artist

(Directly above) **JESSIE STEWART**, *Joy's Market Basket*, 1993. 8" x 12" x 9" (20.3 x 30.5 x 22.9 cm); reed. Designed by Joy Crook. Photo by Blair Logue

Cat-Head Bowl

This basket is a traditional Shaker design. Held bottom up, the silhouette looks
like the head of a cat, the little feet forming ears on the bowl-shaped head.
The basket features a sawtooth rim and dyed stakes to show off the twill weave.
If you don't feel up to weaving a twill, try chase-weave.
Simply start up the sides with two weavers instead of one.

BASIC SKILLS NEEDED	TECHNIQUES YOU'LL LEARN	OTHER SUPPLIES
laying out a base, page 19	continuous 2-1 twill weave	tan basket dye
continuous plain weave, page 12	making a sawtooth rim	

FINISHED SIZE 10 X 10 X 6 INCHES
(25.4 X 25.4 X 15.2 CM)

MATERIALS

QUANTITY	MATERIAL & DIMENSIONS	LENGTH	FUNCTION
14	³/₈" (9.5 mm) flat reed	21" (53.3 cm)	stakes*
	¹/₄" (6 mm) flat-oval reed	55' (16.8 m)	weavers
1	¹/₂" (1.3 cm) flat-oval reed	34" (86.4 cm)	rim
1	¹/₄" (6 mm) flat-oval reed	7' (2.1 m)	lashing

*dye all tan

INSTRUCTIONS

1 Mark the centers of the 14 stakes on the wrong side. Dampen them and align seven in one direction and seven in the other, matching the center marks, and weave them wrong side up in a plain weave. Adjust and square up the base to 4¹/₂ x 4¹/₂ inches (11.4 x 11.4 cm).

2 Use paper shears with long blades to taper your first weaver, cutting it in half lengthwise for at least 7' (2.1 m). Leave the other end full width.

3 Flip the basket base smooth side up so you can work on the outside of the basket bottom. Tuck the tapered end of the ¹/₈-inch (3 mm) weaver down between a horizontal and vertical stake along any side (photo 1). Plain weave for one row around the basket, the oval side of the weaver facing up.

4 After completing the first circle, change to a 2-1 twill weave, weaving over two stakes, then under one. Continue around the base, pulling the weaver snug around the corners. Because the 28 stakes aren't evenly divisible by three, the weave will automatically build up in a twill design.

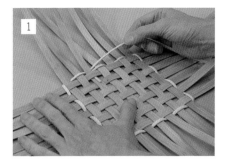

5 After two rows, start pulling together the corner stakes. Clip the stakes together at each corner (photo 2) to help form the "ears." Keep weaving 2-1 as you force the stakes into a starburst (stakes evenly spaced), and the corners will pucker up off the table into "ears" (photos 3 and 4).

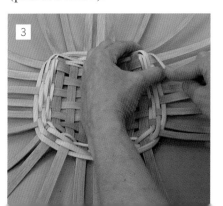

6 Work around the circle until it's 8 inches (20.3 cm) across. Add new weavers as needed with a five-stake overlap, hiding the ends.

7 To shape the bowl, start forcing the sides up by gently bending them without crimping (photo 5). When the bowl is 5 inches (12.7 cm) high, or 2¹/₂ inches (6.4 cm) of stake is still exposed, taper the end of the weaver to a point. End the weave on the same side you began.

8 Even up the basket. Add a traditional lashed rim if the diameter of the basket's top opening is greater than 10 inches (25.4 cm) or less than 8 inches (20.3 cm)—or simply because you want one! If so, refer to page 22 of the Basic Basket, cutting all the pieces long enough to encircle the rim and overlap by 2 inches (5 cm). You can also create a lashed rim without having to tuck any stakes, if the stakes aren't too close together or too far apart.

9 To make the sawtooth rim, soak the stakes. Shave down one end of a piece of ¹/₂-inch (1.3 cm) flat-oval reed and round the tip (this prepares it to be over-lapped by the other end when you finish the rim). Place the shaved end on the outside of the stakes, rounded side facing out. Put the ¹/₄-inch (6 mm) lashing behind a stake to the right of the thinned-down end. This will be the starting stake. Leave a 3-inch (7.6 cm) tail of lashing on the inside of the basket. Hold or clip the rim and lashing in place, and wrap the lashing around the rim, between two stakes, and to the inside (photo 6).

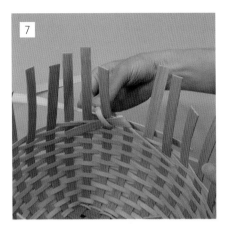

10 Fold the starting stake down and over, behind the next upright stake, working in the direction you're lashing. As the lashing crosses behind the folded-down stake, use it to catch and secure the stake's end. Wrap the lashing around the rim in between the next two stakes (photo 7).

11 Continue folding and wrapping the stakes around the basket (photo 8). Keep them wet and work carefully to prevent cracking.

12 As you complete the circle, thin the loose end of the rim so it fits smoothly against the rim's starting point. To lock in the last stake, thread the lashing up under the first folded stake. Use several more wraps of lashing to overlap the starting point (photo 9). Clip off the lashing tails so they don't show. After the basket is dry, neatly trim the ends of the stakes on the inside of the basket.

Short Cuts Basket

This design is good for using up short leftover pieces of dyed reed. You'll use a technique called French randing, which allows you to weave a large basket while using materials shorter than the basket's diameter. The basket also features a triple-weave structure.

BASIC SKILLS NEEDED
laying out a filled base, page 46
twining, page 19
upsetting, page 20
adding a rim, page 22

TECHNIQUES YOU'LL LEARN
triple-weave
French randing
FINISHED SIZE 6 X 10 X 5 INCHES (15.2 X 25.4 X 12.7 CM)

MATERIALS

QUANTITY	DIMENSION & TYPE	LENGTH	FUNCTION
4	1/2" (1.3 cm) flat reed	25 inches (63.5 cm)	stakes
9	1/2" (1.3 cm) flat reed	19" (48.3 cm)	stakes
3	1/2" (1.3 cm) flat reed	14" (35.6 cm)	fillers
1	#2 round reed	10' (3 m)	twining
	#3 round reed	130' (39.6 m)	weavers
26	assorted widths and colors of reed	9" (22.9 cm)	French-randing*
1	3/8" (9.5 mm) flat reed	32" (81.3 cm)	hidden weaver
2	1/2" (1.3 cm) flat-oval reed	32" (81.3 cm)	rim
1	#3 seagrass	32" (81.3 cm)	rim filler
2	#3 round reed	8' (2.4 m)	lashing

* Use pieces 3/16- to 1/2-inch (5 mm to 1.3 cm) wide, half of the pieces wider, half narrower. The narrower sizes can be flat or flat-oval. If you choose to use only narrow weavers, cut them in 12- to 14-inch (30.5 to 35.6 cm) lengths. That way, your basket will be as tall as the one shown.

INSTRUCTIONS

1 Mark the centers (on the wrong sides) of the 13 stakes and three filler strips. Soak them until pliable and work all materials damp.

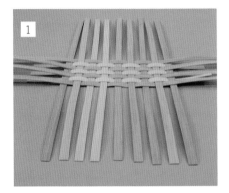

2 Weave the base (photo 1). Alternate the 25-inch (63.5 cm) stakes with the fillers, packing tightly. The 19-inch (48.3 cm) stakes should be $1/2$ inch (1.3 cm) apart. The center 19-inch stake should be on top of the fillers (as is every alternate 19-inch stake). This ensures the filler strips will end up underneath the outer 19-inch stakes.

3 Adjust the bottom to $8^1/2$ x $3^5/8$ inches (21.6 x 9.2 cm). Square up the corners and mark them.

4 Split the center filler strip lengthwise back to the outside stake. Fold it back on itself, over the outside stake, and tuck the ends

under the stakes on either side of the filler (photo 2). Don't split the other two fillers; fold each filler around its adjacent outer stake, then tuck each one under the second stake in, matching it to the split center stake.

5 Now you'll twine around the bottom. Soak the #2 round reed until it's very pliable. Fold a piece of the #2 round reed in half

and place the fold around a stake on a long side of the base. Twine around the base for two rows. Tuck the ends between the layers of the stakes, clipping them off neatly (photo 3).

6 Upsett the stakes by folding and crimping them at the edge of the basket base.

7 Now you'll triple-weave four rows of #3 round reed around the sides of the basket. We haven't used this weave structure before, but it is a very useful technique. Start three pieces of #3 round reed behind three consecutive stakes, one per stake (photo 4). Mark the leftmost stake in this group of three as the beginning stake. While holding the three pieces of round reed in place, weave the leftmost one over two stakes, behind the

third, and back to the outside of the basket (photo 5). Then, release that piece. Repeat, using the newly leftmost piece (photo 6). You'll always use the leftmost weaver to work over the other two. Continue this alternation around the basket, turning up the sides as straight as possible and working toward an oval shape. When four rows are completed and you've returned to the beginning stake, clip off the #3 reed behind the first three stakes (photo 7, page 76).

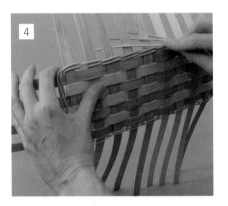

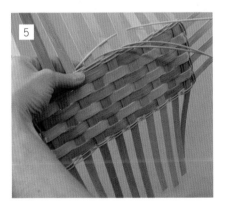

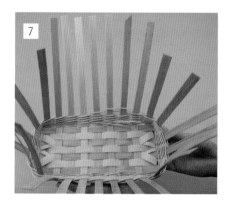

them to the inside. They should end by traveling behind two or three stakes on the inside of the basket (photo 9). There's no way to hide the ends on the inside of the basket, so clip them off as neatly as possible (on a long diagonal, if necessary).

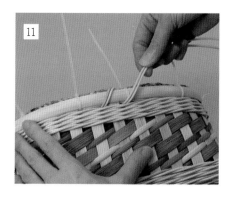

11 This basket has a regular lashed rim. Use the ¹/₂-inch (1.3 cm) flat-oval reed to form the rim and the #3 seagrass for the filler. Use two pieces of the #2 round reed to lash the rim (photo 11), working them just as you would flat reed and making sure they don't twist around each other as you lace them into place.

8 Insert the twenty-six 9-inch (22.9 cm) pieces of dyed reed into the sides of the basket in any order of color and size, intermingling the different widths. Each

9 Using the remaining #3 round reed, add four more rows of triple-weave, starting and stopping as explained in step 7 (photo 10). Make sure the first row is level and doesn't undulate as it circles the basket.

10 Weave one row of plain weave. Use the ³/₈-inch (9.5 mm) flat reed in a start-and-stop weave around the top of the basket. Pack everything down evenly, then fold and tuck the outside stakes to the inside and clip off the inside stakes.

piece should start behind a different stake (photo 8). Using plain weave, work them diagonally up the sides of the basket so they build on each other. Each piece should end behind a different stake. Cut them off at a neat angle while they're on the outside of the basket, then move

Bathroom Catch-Alls

These baskets were inspired by a gift that a friend made for my bathroom. They're sized to sit on a toilet tank and catch clutter. Or, fill them with hand towels and special soaps and display them on a countertop.

BASIC SKILLS NEEDED

laying out a base, page 19

twining, page 19

upsetting, page 20

triple-weave, page 75

adding a rim, page 22

TECHNIQUES YOU'LL LEARN

start-and-stop 2-2 twill weave

FINISHED SIZE 5 X 13 X 3 INCHES
(12.7 X 33 X 7.6 CM)

OTHER SUPPLIES

mauve basket dye

MATERIALS

QUANTITY	MATERIAL & DIMENSIONS	LENGTH	FUNCTION
5	$1/2$" (1.3 cm) flat reed	24" (61 cm)	stakes
13	$1/2$" (1.3 cm) flat reed	16" (40.6 cm)	stakes
1	#2 round reed	8' (2.4 m)	twining
3	#3 round reed	12' (3.6 m)	triple-weave
7	$1/4$" (6 mm) flat reed	43" (109.2 cm)	weavers*
1	$3/8$" (9.5 mm) flat reed	43" (109.2 cm)	hidden weaver
2	$1/2$" (1.3 cm) flat-oval reed	43" (109.2 cm)	rim
1	#6 round reed	43" (109.2 cm)	rim filler
1	$1/4$" (6 mm) flat reed	8' (2.4 m)	lashing

*These weavers should be dyed.

INSTRUCTIONS

1 Mark the centers of the 18 stakes on the wrong sides.

2 Dampen all materials. Plain weave the base, the five 24-inch (61 cm) stakes in one direction and the thirteen 16-inch (40.6 cm) stakes in the other, all facing wrong side up. Match the center points. Adjust the bottom to 12 x 4^1/$_2$ inches (30.5 x 11.4 cm). Square and mark the corners.

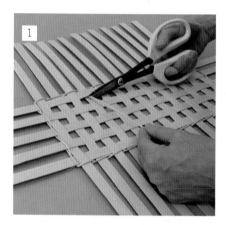

3 Now you'll twine around the bottom. Soak the #2 round reed until it's very pliable. Fold it in half. Place the fold around any stake that lies under a perpendicular stake on a long side of the base. Twine one row around the base. Tuck the ends between the layers of the stakes, clipping them off neatly (photo 1).

4 Upset the stakes by folding and crimping them at the edge of the base.

5 Mark the beginning stake. Using three pieces of the #3 round reed, create four rows of triple-weave (page 74), turning up the sides. (You should be working on the outside of the basket.)

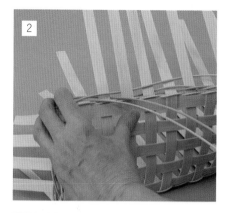

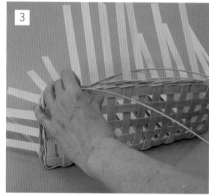

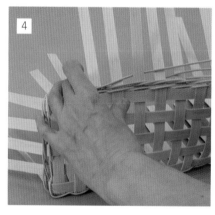

6 You may have noticed the little pattern break at the beginning and end of the triple-weave in the Short Cuts Basket (page 74). You can avoid this by using a process called "stepping up" once between each round. Stop weaving when the leading weaver is to the left of the beginning stake. You will continue to weave over two, under one, and out, but you'll step up to the next round by starting with the leading weaver instead of the trailing one. Weave it over two, under one, and out (photo 2). Put it down and

repeat the same pattern with the next weaver to the left (photo 3). Put that weaver down and do the same thing with the third weaver (photo 4). Now your "step up" is complete and you're ready to triple-weave this round, again using the trailing weaver first. Repeat between each round.

7 To end the triple-weave, stop when the leading weaver is to the left of the beginning stake, weave it over two and in, and leave it inside the basket. Repeat with the next weaver to the left, then the remaining weaver. Clip off the weavers so they lie flat against successive stakes.

8 Use paper shears to split all the stakes in half lengthwise.

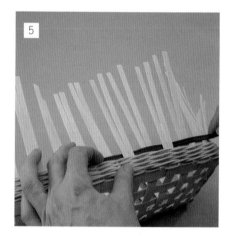

9 You'll use the seven pieces of dyed ^{1}/$_4$-inch (6 mm) flat reed to twill-weave up the sides of your basket. Though you're weaving 2-2 instead of 1-1, it's still a start-and-stop weave. Each half of the ^{1}/$_2$-inch (1.3 cm) flat reed stakes should be considered an individual stake. Weave the first row over and under the split pairs of stakes (photo 5). Overlap by eight stakes (four pairs) to hide the ends.

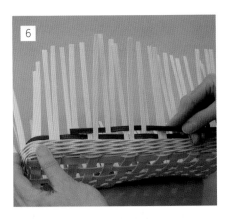

10 Weave the second row 2-2, but start one stake to the right (photo 6). You may have to pull apart the pairs to open enough space between the stakes to accommodate weavers.

11 Now weave each row, starting one stake over to the right, making little stair-step diagonals. You can start on any side of the basket; just make sure the weave advances one stake to the right on each row. The basket may tend to warp because of its long, narrow shape, so pay attention to keeping the bottom flat.

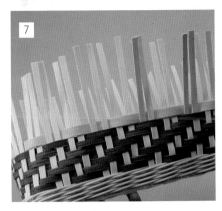

12 Weave in the hidden weaver, using $3/8$" (9.5 mm) flat reed. Weave 2-2, but alternate with the row below (photo 7).

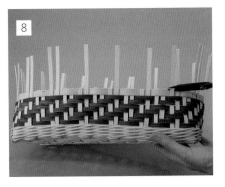

13 Clip off all the stakes that end on the inside of the hidden weaver, and clip off one of each pair that ends on the outside (photo 8). Fold and tuck the remaining stakes.

14 Use the $1/2$" (1.3 cm) flat-oval reed to form the rim and #6 round reed for the filler, then lash it between the split pairs.

15 To make basket number two, reverse the twill steps after the fourth row (photo 9).

Conclusion

If you've worked through all the baskets here, congratulations! You're no longer a beginner, and you're ready to start designing your own baskets. Spend time looking at baskets whenever you can and figure out how they were constructed. Let them inspire and educate you. Decide on methods that work well for you and abandon the ones that don't. But most of all enjoy the process!

ACKNOWLEDGMENTS

First, I would like to thank Lark Crafts and Sterling Publishing for giving me the opportunity to write this book and for waiting for me to fit it into my schedule. I would also like to thank my extended family and the Earth Guild crew for their support, understanding, and the space they made available. This book would not have happened without their help. A special thanks goes to Esther Holsen, who pushed, prodded, and poked me into photo shoots when I would have put them off "until next week." Without her standing by and photographing each basket as I made it, I would have had a much more difficult time showing readers everything I wanted them to see about the process of making baskets. And thanks, too, to my husband, Bud, for everything he does to make my life more interesting.

INDEX

GALLERY ARTISTS

Dianne Kennedy Craver enjoys working with her hands and finds that weaving baskets soothes her after a stressful day. She lives in Asheville, North Carolina.

Donna Sakamoto Crispin resides in Eugene, Oregon. When weaving with reed and cane, she adds materials closer to their natural states for interest and texture.

Patti Hawkins has taught and exhibited basketry nationally since 1986. Her work features geometric shapes, layering, and creative use of color, but her first love remains the rhythm of twill weaving. She lives in Prattville, Alabama.

Patti Quinn Hill is a member of the Southern Highland Craft Guild and many national organizations. Her work has appeared in books on wreath making, beadwork, and basketry. She lives in Weaverville, North Carolina.

Alma Lambert teaches basket weaving at a community college in Asheville, North Carolina, where she also lives.

Blair Logue is a professional weaver and also teaches basketry. An owner of Earth Guild, she lives on 300 acres of mountain woodland outside Asheville, North Carolina.

Helen Schwartz changed her focus from painting and printmaking the moment she wove her first basket. The patterns and textures of her work often resemble textiles. She lives in Princeton, New Jersey.

Mary Young Smith works primarily with round reed, willow, and honeysuckle. She also knits and weaves and teaches all three crafts. She lives in Asheville, North Carolina.

Jessie Stewart has taught basketry but now weaves baskets as a hobby to keep her mind and hands busy. She is a longtime resident of Candler, North Carolina.

Linda Arter Sura creates baskets using both traditional and unusual materials, including wire, feathers, beads, and reeds. She owns Lagniappe Weavers, a basket and gourd supply business in Slidell, Louisiana.

Angie Wagner owns Woven Branch Designs in Landsdale, Pennsylvania. She designs her baskets with the idea that everyone needs an attractive place to catch all their clutter.

Shannon Weber has created baskets so large she can't get them out of her studio. Clad only in undergarments, she once forded a snowy river to gather some willow, and she also escaped a speeding ticket when the officer noticed a basket in her car's backseat. She lives in Westfir, Oregon.